# CRASH
## FROM
# OUTER SPACE

UNRAVELING THE MYSTERY OF **FLYING SAUCERS**,
**ALIEN BEINGS**, AND **ROSWELL**

# CRASH
## FROM
## OUTER SPACE

UNRAVELING THE MYSTERY OF **FLYING SAUCERS**,
**ALIEN BEINGS**, AND **ROSWELL**

## CANDACE FLEMING

SCHOLASTIC INC.

Library of Congress Cataloging-in-Publication Data available

ISBN 978-1-338-86739-8

10 9 8 7 6 5 4 3 2 1    22 23 24 25 26
Printed in the U.S.A.    40
Originally published in hardcover by Scholastic Focus, October 2022
This edition first printing, 2022

Book design by Keirsten Geise

To Max, reader extraordinaire!

# CRASH
## FROM
# OUTER SPACE

UNRAVELING THE MYSTERY OF **FLYING SAUCERS**,
**ALIEN BEINGS**, AND **ROSWELL**

# TABLE OF CONTENTS

# PART 1

*Something Crashed . . .*
*but What?*

## What's That in the Sky?

On the evening of June 13, 1947, William "Mack" Brazel sat on the porch of his tiny ranch house near Roswell, New Mexico. After a long, hot day of hard work, the cool stillness of the desert night was a welcome relief. Relaxing, Brazel looked out across the vast expanse of the sky.

On the horizon, a storm brewed. Bolts of jagged lightning flashed and flashed again, illuminating a mass of thick, swirling clouds. Brazel leaned forward. In his thirty years as a sheep rancher, he'd seen plenty of New Mexico storms. But he'd never seen anything like this. The storm clouds had turned

Mack Brazel in 1947.

blood red, and lightning kept striking the same spot over and over. The thunderclaps sounded like explosions.

The sky ignited!

Like fireworks, rays of orange and red spread out across the sky. For a moment, the flat terrain of the desert came into stark relief. Brazel could see the sagebrush and cacti as clearly as if it were daytime. Then it was dark again. And a single, fiery object—seemingly from outer space—came whirling and twisting, plummeting to Earth. Seconds later there was a burst of brilliant light. Something had crashed out there. But what?

Brazel dismissed the idea of it being a meteorite. The object had been too big. Instead, he suspected that a military plane had gone down. Or maybe, some sort of secret weapon was being tested out there. Lots of strange things had been seen in New Mexico's skies over the past few years. Brazel, like most folks around Roswell, figured they were part of the US military's "hush-hush" experiments.

New Mexico, with its scrubby, largely empty acres, was a hotbed for the creation of top secret military weapons. At the south end of Roswell stood the Roswell Army Air Field, where the fighting 509th Bomb Wing—the world's only combat unit trained to drop nuclear bombs—practiced. About 100 miles west of Roswell at Alamogordo, the first atomic bomb explosion had shot up its mushroom cloud just two years earlier. Then, of course, there was the Los Alamos Laboratory just three hours north. This was where scientists had developed the first atomic bomb, and where they now worked on nuclear weapons with the potential for a thousand times more explosive power. What's more, outside Albuquerque, at Sandia Base, the military was working on creating atomic bombs the size of hand grenades. And although secrecy shrouded the activities at White Sands Proving Ground and

Missile Range—a two-hour drive from Roswell—it was common knowledge that many of the nation's classified weapons were housed there.

The military's obsession with nuclear weapons stemmed from World War II. A nightmarish conflict that had ended just two years earlier, it had pitted the Allies led by America, the United Kingdom, and the Soviet Union (now Russia) against the main partners in the Axis alliance—Germany, Italy, and Japan. Fighting had occurred all over the globe, and had left sixty million people dead. Even after peace was proclaimed, the world's nations remained tense. The worst friction, however, was between the United States and the Soviet Union. During the war, they had been partners. But now they were competitors, each vying to be *the* superpower in the world. By 1947, a "cold war" existed between them, as each feared the other would start World War III. And that conflict, US military leaders believed, would be fought with nuclear bombs.

So far, the United States alone possessed this fearsome weapon. America had dropped atomic

The United States government perfected its atomic weapons after World War II in the vast emptiness of the American Southwest. Here, in 1951, members of the 11th Airborne Division kneel on the ground to watch a mushroom cloud from a nearby atomic bomb test.

V-2 rockets are launched at White Sands Proving Ground and Missile Range in 1947 as part of the government's classified-weapons program.

bombs—more powerful than anything previously made by humankind—on the Japanese cities of Hiroshima and Nagasaki in August 1945. The bombs had essentially vaporized both cities, and killed a quarter of a million people. American military leaders knew it would not be long before the Soviet Union developed their own nuclear weapons. How best to face down this new enemy? The answer seemed obvious: America needed even more advanced technologies to fight future wars. And that meant science had to be on the frontline. Experimenting. Innovating. Creating.

More bombs.

More missiles.

The 509th Bomb Wing's insignia includes a mushroom cloud, a reminder that it is the only unit trained to drop nuclear bombs.

More secret weapons that would sow terror in the hearts of Soviet leaders.

Mack Brazel watched the pulsing red glow on the horizon until it faded to black. What had just crashed out there? He'd find out tomorrow.

## ✧ 2 ✧

## What Is It?

Mack Brazel headed out at dawn the next morning. Beside him in his pickup truck sat his eight-year-old son, Vernon, and his fourteen-year-old daughter, Bessie. Because the ranch was so isolated, there were no paved roads. Brazel simply put the truck into drive, and barreled across the hard-packed desert sand.

A couple miles from the ranch house, the truck crested a lonely rise. Brazel braked. He and the kids climbed out. For a moment they just stood and stared. What was all that stuff?

Strange-looking debris lay strewn across the field. There were small lightweight sticks the color and texture of balsa wood, only stronger;

The vast and mostly empty New Mexico landscape where Mack Brazel and his kids found mysterious debris.

pieces of hard, black plastic; lengths of something that looked like fishing line; and a material that appeared to be parchment paper. Most fascinating were the numerous pieces of grayish-silver metallic foil. Ranging in size from a few inches to three or more feet across, they rustled like dry leaves in the hot desert wind.

Bewildered, the family moved closer. Bessie noticed a lightweight metal beam with some of the foil-like material attached to it. Etched into the material were pink and purple symbols. It appeared to be some kind of writing, although they couldn't read it. Bessie thought the symbols looked like Egyptian hieroglyphs. Vernon thought they just looked like scribbles.

Incredibly, Mack Brazel didn't seem to particularly care about what the stuff was, or where it had come from. Mostly, he felt annoyed at the mess. It would be a job to pick up all the pieces. Still, his sheep hadn't been harmed, and that's what really mattered. He shooed the kids back into the truck. They would deal with this mess later. Right now, they had chores to do.

## ✧ 3 ✧

## What Could It Be?

Ten days later, on June 24, 1947, amateur pilot Kenneth Arnold climbed into his two-seater airplane and took off from Chehalis, Washington, for an air show in Pendleton, Oregon. The afternoon sky was clear; there was a light breeze.

As he neared Washington's Mount Rainier, he banked toward the south for a closer look. A Marine Corps C-46 transport had crashed in the area recently, and the military was offering a $5,000 reward to the person who found the wreckage. Arnold doubted he'd see anything. Still, it was worth a flyover.

As he looked out his side window, there came a bright light—just a flash—like a "mirror reflecting sunlight at me," Arnold later recalled. It had a strange, bluish tinge. Was the light coming from a nearby plane? Arnold thought so. He looked around, but saw nothing.

The light came again, this time in a series. Nine flashes.

*Blink-blink-blink-blink-blink-blink-blink-blink-blink!*

That's when he saw them—to his left—nine sparkling objects flying in a diagonal-shaped formation. Arnold, who'd been a pilot in World War II, recognized the formation. It was an advance military tactic, used to break through enemy lines.

What Arnold *didn't* recognize was the aircraft.

The objects came closer, flying between him and the snow-covered mountain peak.

Now Arnold could see they were crescent shaped. As he watched in amazement, they flipped and banked, darting around like "the tail of a kite" yet moving in unison. No plane Arnold had ever encountered moved like that. He wondered if he was witnessing the test flight of some secret military aircraft. He decided to clock their speed by calculating how long it took them to get from Mount Rainier to Mount Adams, a distance of fifty miles.

The objects covered the distance in just one minute and forty-two seconds.

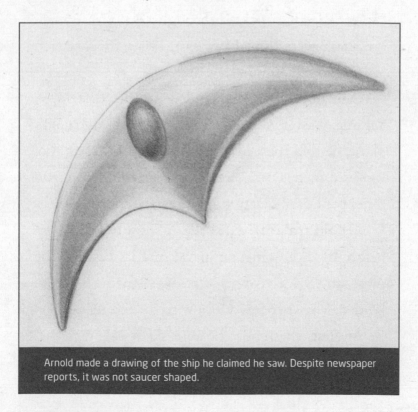

Arnold made a drawing of the ship he claimed he saw. Despite newspaper reports, it was not saucer shaped.

Arnold did the math and came up with an astonishing answer: 1,700 miles per hour. How could that be? This was faster than the speed of sound, and three times faster than any aircraft's capability at the time. (By comparison, the fastest commercial passenger jet manufactured today has a top speed of 660 miles per hour). He felt suddenly cold, and "an eerie feeling" passed through his body.

The objects zipped away.

A stunned Arnold flew on.

One hour later, he landed at the airstrip in Yakima, Washington. As mechanics refueled Arnold's plane, he told them about his experience. They, too, were stunned. Flying crescents that could go 1,700 miles per hour? *That* was a tale worth repeating.

Arnold's tale arrived at the airshow in Pendleton before he did. Someone in Yakima had called the press, and a clutch of reporters was waiting when he landed. They peppered him with questions.

At first, the reporters were skeptical. Was this guy some kind of crackpot? But Arnold, a respected businessman and experienced pilot, won them over with his calm retelling. The pilot didn't exaggerate or sensationalize his story. As he relayed what he'd seen, he gave the impression of being a careful observer. When the reporters filed their news stories, they treated the sighting as serious, credible news.

Like summer lightning, reports of Arnold's sighting flashed across the country. People from Maine to California read about it on the front pages of their newspapers. Press accounts used "flying saucer" to describe the crafts' shape. This, however, was *not* how Arnold had described them. He'd said the objects *flew* "like a saucer skipping across the water." The objects were actually "thin and crescent-shaped."

This misquote, however, stuck. The concept of "flying saucers" was transferred to a fascinated nation almost overnight, and became a household phrase. A Gallup poll taken just six weeks after Arnold's sighting discovered that 90 percent of Americans had heard the term "flying saucer." UFOs had entered the culture.

Kenneth Arnold is photographed in 1947 in front of his airplane shortly after reporting seeing nine high-speed flying objects.

People everywhere started scanning the skies. And many claimed they found what they were looking for. In the six months after Arnold's sighting, 853 flying disc sightings were reported. They came from every state in the US, as well as Canada.

Were they flying saucers from outer space?

And if so, why were they suddenly visiting Earth?

A group of Americans gather in a Michigan pasture to search the night sky for UFOs.

## ✧ 4 ✧

## Could It *Really* Be a Flying Saucer?

Mack Brazel hadn't been back to the debris site in nearly three weeks. But on Friday, July 4, he returned with his wife, Maggie, as well as Vernon and Bessie. Excitedly, the kids raced around picking up handfuls of the silvery material and shoving them into the empty wool sacks they'd brought along. According to Bessie, they gathered up "quite a bit of the debris" before heading home.

Later that day, Brazel drove the thirty miles to the home of his closest neighbors, Floyd and Loretta

Proctor. The three sat around the kitchen table chatting and sipping coffee for a while. Then Brazel brought out a few pieces of the debris. One piece—tan colored, pencil sized, and lighter than a feather— baffled the Proctors. "He couldn't cut it, or tear it," claimed Loretta Proctor. "And it wouldn't burn when Mack held a lit match to it." Another piece, she recalled, "looked like aluminum foil, [but] crumple it and it would go back to its [original] shape."

Floyd Proctor suggested Brazel report his find to officials in Roswell. Loretta agreed. If it came from the sky, she bet it had something to do with the military. Surely, officers at the Roswell Army Air Field would want to know about it.

Brazel, however, didn't see the need to notify authorities. Besides, he didn't own a phone. Neither did the Proctors. To talk with the sheriff, he'd have to drive the eighty-five miles into Roswell. And Brazel certainly didn't want to do that on a Saturday night. Instead, he drove to nearby Corona to meet a couple of buddies for supper.

Over burgers and beers, he mentioned the debris he'd found.

His friends grew excited. Maybe he'd found parts of a downed flying saucer!

A *what*?

"Flying saucer," they repeated. Reports of them had been on the radio and in the newspapers for weeks, ever since a pilot named Kenneth Arnold reportedly spotted nine unidentified flying objects over Mount Rainier. It was big news. Hadn't Mack heard about it?

Brazel hadn't. He'd been out on his remote sheep ranch without radio or newspaper. He hadn't heard a thing about flying saucers . . . until now.

But he still didn't think it was worth making a special trip to Roswell. He planned on going into town on Monday to sell some wool. His discovery would just have to wait until then.

Mid-morning on Monday, July 7, Mack Brazel turned onto Roswell's main street. Roswell was the nearest thing to a big city in this part of New Mexico. The county seat, it boasted an ornate domed courthouse, as well as the New Mexico Military Institute, a boarding school for boys. It also had a three-story hotel called the Nickson, two radio stations, the Hotpoint Movie Theater, five churches, Ballard Funeral Home, the Busy Bee Café, two local newspapers, and the Chaves County Sheriff Station.

An aerial view of Roswell, New Mexico, taken around the time Mack Brazel reported his find to the county sheriff.

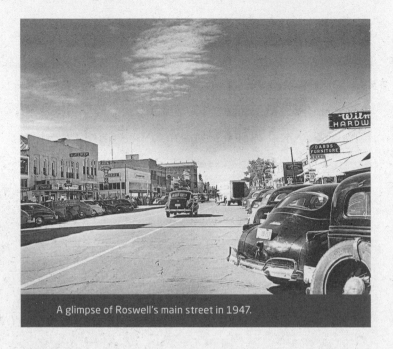

A glimpse of Roswell's main street in 1947.

Brazel had brought along a few pieces of debris. Now he laid them on Sheriff George Wilcox's desk. Could they be part of a flying saucer?

Wilcox examined the stuff. Maybe. Who was to say?

The sheriff's phone rang. On the line was Frank Joyce, an announcer and news reporter at radio station KGFL. Joyce called the station every morning, looking for a news scoop. Had Wilcox arrested anyone last night? Had he been called to any crime scenes?

Most days, Wilcox said no. Not much out of the ordinary happened in sleepy Roswell. But today, to Joyce's surprise, the sheriff had something for him. He put Brazel on the line.

The rancher told him about the debris.

Despite all the press about flying saucers, Joyce didn't think Brazel's debris was newsworthy. If something really had fallen out of the sky, he said, it had most likely come from the nearby airfield. Joyce suggested they call over there.

Wilcox did. He was put through to the 509th Bomb Squadron's intelligence officer, Major Jesse A. Marcel.

Again, Brazel told his story.

Major Marcel listened closely. Obviously, the matter didn't sound too urgent, because instead of heading right over to the sheriff's office, he went to lunch at the officer's club. It wasn't until mid-afternoon that he went to see Wilcox.

The debris pieces still lay on the sheriff's desk. Marcel looked them over. They were, he agreed, peculiar. Pocketing a few pieces, he returned to the base. He showed them to his commanding officer, Colonel William H. Blanchard.

Blanchard had never seen anything like them. Could some experimental aircraft have crashed? Classified programs, top secret tests and trust-no-one security defined the Cold War. Therefore, strange events in sensitive areas like Roswell caused alarm. There were so *many* military secrets. Nobody knew everything that was going on. Blanchard decided the incident required immediate investigation. He ordered Marcel to get out to the ranch right away.

Marcel went, taking with him another intelligence officer, Captain Sheridan Cavitt. The men followed Brazel out to the debris site. To Marcel's surprise, it was smaller than he had expected, just "three quarters of a mile long and two hundred to three hundred feet wide." He noted how the debris lay in a fanlike shape, running northwest to south-west, and how it appeared nothing had actually hit the ground. "It was something that must have exploded above the ground and fell," Marcel later recalled. To confirm his observation, he checked the surrounding area. He found "no fresh impact depression in the sand."

Back at the base, Blanchard was placing a phone call to his superiors. The material could be from some top secret program, he said. How would they like him to proceed? The matter quickly traveled up the chain of command to Strategic Air Command at Andrews Army Air Field outside Washington, DC. There, a higher-up ordered that the material brought into town by Brazel be flown to him. By dinnertime, a B-29 bomber with a sealed bag of the debris aboard was winging its way to the nation's capital.

Back at the ranch, Marcel and Cavitt were running out of daylight. Leaving the wreckage site, they returned to Brazel's house. The rancher hauled the debris-stuffed wool sacks from the shed where he'd stored them. These contained the pieces Vernon and Bessie had picked up days earlier. Now, the kids watched wide-eyed as Marcel ran a Geiger counter over the pieces. To everyone's relief, they didn't hear the loud crackling that indicated the presence of radiation.

Next, Marcel and Cavitt attempted to fit the debris pieces together. "They tried to make a kite out of it," recalled Brazel. Indeed, that's exactly what the debris looked like—the leftovers of a huge, wrecked kite. Brazel, however, didn't think that's what it was. He also didn't think the debris had come from a weather balloon as Marcel now suggested. Twice before, the rancher had found the remains of weather balloons on his land, and this stuff looked different. But that *didn't* mean he thought the debris had come from a flying saucer. "When [it] was all gathered up, the tinfoil, paper, tape and sticks made a bundle about 3 feet long, and 7 or 8 inches thick, while the rubber made a bundle about 18 or 20 inches long and about 8 inches thick. [The] entire lot maybe weighed five pounds." There was also, noted Brazel, "considerable scotch tape and some tape with flowers printed upon it . . . that had been used in the construction."

A flying saucer stuck together with Scotch tape? Not likely.

No, this was something else . . . wasn't it?

## ✧ 5 ✧

## Is Anyone Telling the Truth?

It was past midnight by the time Marcel and Cavitt returned to the Roswell Army Air Field with the debris-stuffed wool sacks. Intelligence agents were called into Blanchard's office to examine the wreckage. Had some secret testing or exercise gone awry? No one knew.

But Colonel Blanchard already had his orders. The material was to be sent to Brigadier General Roger Ramey, commander of the Eighth Army Air Force District at the Fort Worth Army Base. And so, hours later, the bags were put aboard a second B-29 and flown to Texas. Major Marcel accompanied them.

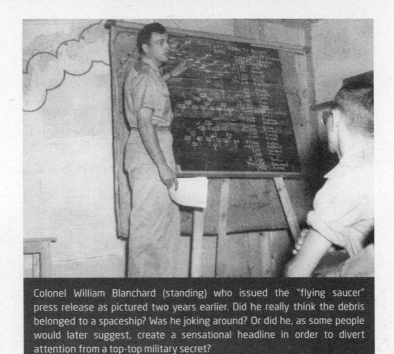

Colonel William Blanchard (standing) who issued the "flying saucer" press release as pictured two years earlier. Did he really think the debris belonged to a spaceship? Was he joking around? Or did he, as some people would later suggest, create a sensational headline in order to divert attention from a top-top military secret?

It was now Tuesday morning, July 8. Public Relations Officer Walter Haut was just sitting down at his desk for the day when his telephone rang. It was Colonel Blanchard. And he wanted Haut to issue a press release. It said:

*"The many rumors regarding the flying disc became reality yesterday when the intelligence*

*office of the 509th Bomb Group . . . was fortunate enough to gain possession of a disc through the cooperation of one of the local ranchers and the sheriff's office of Chaves County. The flying object landed on a ranch near Roswell sometime last week. Not having phone facilities, the rancher stored the disc until such time as he was able to contact the sheriff's office . . . action was immediately taken and the disc was picked up. It was inspected at Roswell Army Air Field and*

Public Relations Officer Walter Haut in 1947. He would later claim that issuing a press release about capturing a flying saucer wasn't, to his mind, out of the ordinary.

*subsequently [sent] by Major Marcel to higher headquarters."*

Incredibly, Haut didn't seem surprised by the press release. "There were quite a few reports of flying saucers at that time," he later recalled, and "I had all kinds of things to do [on base]." And so he typed up the release, made copies, and sent it to Roswell's two radio stations, KSWS and KGFL, as well as its two newspapers, the *Roswell Daily Record* and the *Roswell Daily Dispatch*.

The front page headline of the *Roswell Daily Record* for July 8, 1947, shouts the news: the Army Air Force has caught a flying saucer!

KSWS immediately put the news on the air, and then phoned it in to the Associate Press Bureau in Albuquerque. Soon after, KGFL aired the story. National interest exploded. Phone calls from news outlets all across the country swamped the sheriff's office, as well as the Roswell Army Air Force Field's public relations office. Haut felt sideswiped. He hadn't expected this kind of response. He didn't expect the phone call he received that afternoon from the War Department either. They bluntly ordered him to "shut up."

While the nation's press chased the story, Captain Cavitt returned to the debris site with Major Sergeant Lewis Rickett. A handful of military policemen had already secured the site. Not that there was much left to protect. Only a small portion of the wreckage remained. "Maybe forty or fifty small pieces," recalled Rickett. It was clear, however, that whatever the stuff was, it was very "hush-hush."

Meanwhile, at the Fort Worth Army Base, General Ramey called a press conference. Just hours earlier, Public Relations Officer Haut had told the press

Major Jesse Marcel poses for newspaper reporters with a piece of the foil-lined material found by Mack Brazel.

General Roger Ramey poses for reporters with Major Marcel and more of the debris. Notice how the pieces, when put together, resemble a kite.

that a flying disc had been found. But now the military changed its story. Broadcasting over the radio, Ramey explained to listeners that the so-called flying disc was nothing more than a weather balloon. "As far as I can see there is nothing to get excited about," he added. He then invited reporters into his office to see the debris. Both he and Marcel posed with pieces of it while news photographers snapped away.

Is this contraption the source of the strange debris? The Army Air Force claimed it was. Here, airmen attach a radar device to a weather balloon just prior to liftoff at Fort Worth Air Base in July 1947.

Back in Roswell, Mack Brazel was also talking with reporters. He took the opportunity to correct the base's press release. He'd found the wreckage *three* weeks earlier, he stressed, not a week ago as officials stated. No, the stuff didn't look like it had come from outer space. It was scraps of foil, wood, "rather tough paper," and rubber. There was also some "tape with flowers printed on it."

Brazel didn't act excited about the discovery. He didn't act as if it was anything out of the ordinary.

The front page of *Roswell Daily Record* for July 9, 1947, announces the sudden change in the Army Air Force's story.

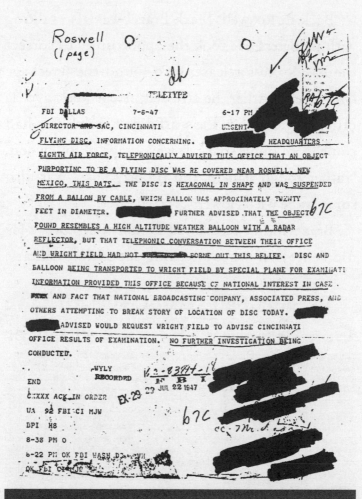

Roswell
(1 page)

TELETYPE

FBI DALLAS            7-8-47              6-17 PM

DIRECTOR AND SAC, CINCINNATI          URGENT

FLYING DISC. INFORMATION CONCERNING.          HEADQUARTERS

EIGHTH AIR FORCE, TELEPHONICALLY ADVISED THIS OFFICE THAT AN OBJECT

PURPORTING TO BE A FLYING DISC WAS RE COVERED NEAR ROSWELL, NEW

MEXICO, THIS DATE. THE DISC IS HEXAGONAL IN SHAPE AND WAS SUSPENDED

FROM A BALLON BY CABLE, WHICH BALLON WAS APPROXIMATELY TWENTY

FEET IN DIAMETER.          FURTHER ADVISED THAT THE OBJECT

FOUND RESEMBLES A HIGH ALTITUDE WEATHER BALLOON WITH A RADAR

REFLECTOR, BUT THAT TELEPHONIC CONVERSATION BETWEEN THEIR OFFICE

AND WRIGHT FIELD HAD NOT          BORNE OUT THIS BELIEF. DISC AND

BALLOON BEING TRANSPORTED TO WRIGHT FIELD BY SPECIAL PLANE FOR EXAMINATI

INFORMATION PROVIDED THIS OFFICE BECAUSE OF NATIONAL INTEREST IN CASE

AND FACT THAT NATIONAL BROADCASTING COMPANY, ASSOCIATED PRESS, AND

OTHERS ATTEMPTING TO BREAK STORY OF LOCATION OF DISC TODAY.

ADVISED WOULD REQUEST WRIGHT FIELD TO ADVISE CINCINNATI

OFFICE RESULTS OF EXAMINATION. NO FURTHER INVESTIGATION BEING

CONDUCTED.

                    WYLY
END            RECORDED

CXXXX ACK IN ORDER          EX-29      29 JUL 22 1947

UA  9½ FBI CI MJW

BPI  H8

8-38 PM O

6-22 PM OK FBI WASH DC

OK FBI

Little did the public know that while they focused on the hoopla, the FBI was quietly looking into the strange debris and the purported flying saucer. On July 8, 1947, they wrote this memo to military officials advising that the wreckage looked like it belonged to a high-altitude weather balloon. "No further investigation being conducted," they concluded.

And yet, toward the end of the interview, he said something curious: "I am sure what I found was not any weather balloon." Did he think General Ramey's explanation for the wreckage wasn't true?

The next morning, Wednesday, July 9, Brazel's interview appeared on the front page of the newspaper alongside an article titled "FLYING DISK EXPLAINED."

That seemed to be that. The military considered the Roswell case closed. And the press regarded the story as over. After all, there wasn't anything more to tell, right?

# PART 2

## Are They Watching
## from Space?

## ✧ 6 ✧

## Little Green Men from Venus . . . Really?

They were loose in the desert . . . little green men . . . from Venus!

So claimed the *Aztec* [New Mexico] *Independent-Review*.

In August 1948, the newspaper's editor decided to play a hoax on his readers. He falsely reported that a flying saucer had crashed on the outskirts of town, and that sixteen Venusians had streamed from the wreckage. The public should be on the lookout.

The story quickly spread. Newspapers around the country ran it on their front pages. And

MATCH THE PICTURES

DON'T TOUCH UNLESS          TOLD TO DO SO

Atomic Bombing Care

TURN

So worried were Americans about an atomic bombing that children-friendly instructions like this one were printed and circulated. Here kids learn not to touch anything after a bombing—not even food or water—unless given permission by a grown-up. Survival depended upon avoiding any fallout from nuclear radiation.

Backyard fallout shelters like this one sprang up across the United States as more and more Americans feared atomic attack. Here, a child and her father practice getting in and out of their underground shelter.

thousands of readers believed it. Panicked, they called their newspaper offices.

Where were the creatures now?

Was the military trying to catch them?

Could Venusians take over the world?

Their response showed how deeply paranoid Americans were feeling. Rapid developments in science and technology had changed the world

45

overnight. What had once been science fiction—rockets, radar, atomic bombs—was now real life. The notion of little green men in spaceships no longer seemed farfetched.

Neither did a Soviet nuclear attack. Since war's end, the Soviet Union had tightened its grip in Eastern Europe, taking over East Germany, Poland, Hungary, and Czechoslovakia. Was the United States next?

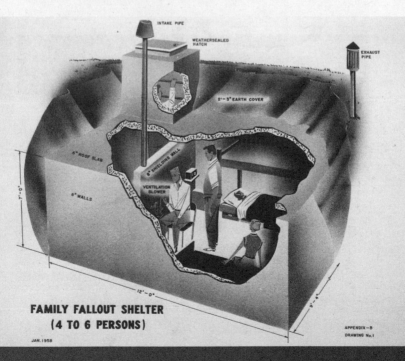

Drawing of a 1958 backyard, underground fallout shelter designed to accommodate a family of six.

Suddenly, watching the sky felt necessary for US survival. Any day now, Soviet bombers might appear overhead. So might an attack from outer space. It seemed as if invasion and annihilation could come from anywhere.

A flurry of conflicting information about UFOs only exacerbated these fears. A two-part feature article

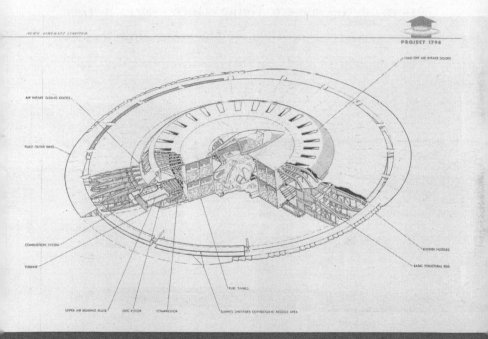

While claiming that flying saucers were too silly to discuss, the Air Force was busy trying to build their own saucer, as this 1956 building plan shows. Throughout the 1950s, the Air Force funded Project 1794, a secret program meant to build a supersonic flying saucer that could spin through the earth's atmosphere at 2,600 miles an hour, rise to heights of 100,000 feet, take off and land vertically, and hover over battlefields. Could some citizen sightings have been of this military secret?

in the national magazine *Saturday Evening Post* dismissed flying saucers as nonsense. Popular newspaper columnist Walter Winchell asserted the sightings were actually Soviet aircraft. And *Fate*, a magazine about the strange and unknown, ran a series of articles about ordinary people who'd had UFO encounters.

Meanwhile, the Air Force issued its official position on the subject: flying saucers were neither extraterrestrial, nor Soviet. They were simply cases of misidentification, and were caused by things like

The VZ-9 Avrocar, pictured here, was the result of Project 1794's efforts. It would have changed the face of air combat if it had worked. It didn't. Designers could never get the Avrocar to rise more than five or six feet off the ground. The Air Force gave up on the flying saucer in 1960.

weird cloud formations, meteors, or even large hail-stones. Saucers from outer space DID NOT EXIST. In fact, officials went so far as to publicly announce that they saw no reason to even *discuss* UFOs. They were, officials claimed, nothing to get excited about.

The Air Force's nonchalance did little to soothe American nerves. Reports of saucer sightings streamed in. They were spied above farmhouses and high school football fields and drive-in movie theaters. They were spotted above tiny towns and big cities. They seemed to be everywhere. But what were they . . . *really?*

On March 8, 1950, a mysterious guest lecturer arrived at the University of Denver. Calling himself "Mr. X," he spoke to a lecture hall full of science students for almost an hour. His remarks left heads spinning.

Spaceships had already landed on Earth, he claimed, four discs that used "lines of magnetic force" as their power source. This made the discs' speed "virtually unlimited." The first disc crashed, and inside it the government had found sixteen extraterrestrial bodies. All were male, between the ages of thirty-five and forty, "if the earth's gauge of time is employed," Mr. X added. Contrary to common belief, they were not green, but had a fair complexion. In fact, they looked just like humans except smaller.

Some of the students laughed at this. Others leaned forward, listening closely.

Mr. X went on. The fourth saucer, he said, had been accidentally discovered by a group of scientists near a government weapons facility. The craft stood empty, but nearby they saw several "little men." The scientists gave chase, but the alien beings escaped.

The students wanted to know what became of the saucer.

"It disappeared," said Mr. X dramatically.

Both murmurs and snickers ran through the room.

Where, and when had all this happened?

The lecturer would not say. But he did hold up a sample of "indestructible [extraterrestrial] material" from which the saucer was made. When a student in the front row held out his hand to touch it, Mr. X put it back into his pocket.

This re-creation at Roswell's International UFO Museum and Research Center shows a crashed flying saucer complete with "little men."

What were the names of the scientists working with the government?

Mr. X named only one: Dr. Gee. He went on to describe how Dr. Gee had been asked by the military to examine both discs and the bodies of alien beings. It was from him, said Mr. X, that he'd learned the truth about flying saucers.

No, he would not reveal Dr. Gee's real name. That might put the scientist in danger. Everything the students had just heard was top secret. If the government learned who had passed on these secrets, well, there was no telling what might happen.

With that, Mr. X thanked them for their attention, and left.

The students buzzed.

Some declared the lecture "electrifying," and "spellbinding."

Others dismissed it as "absurd" and "unbelievable."

Their professor, Francis Broman, moved to the front of the room. He suggested they evaluate what they'd just heard. As future scientists, this would be a good lesson in critical thinking. Did Mr. X meet their tests for "valuable information?" he asked. Dr. Broman reminded the students of the criteria for weighing evidence:

"Did the speaker have firsthand information?"

"Was he an expert in the subject upon which he spoke?"

"Had the information he presented been openly and carefully studied by other experts?"

The students answered no to each of these questions.

It didn't matter that the stories were exciting or that Mr. X sounded believable when he told them. That didn't mean they were true.

Some of the students *wanted* to believe Mr. X. But that didn't make his statements true either.

The class came to the obvious conclusion: Mr. X's story was baloney.

Still, it *was* sensational. The next day, the *Denver Post* reported on the lecture. Within days it became the subject of a syndicated feature article that appeared in hundreds of newspapers across the country. Mr. X's claims caused a stir. To many, it seemed there was more to flying saucers than the Air Force was letting on. Many Americans wondered: What *was* the truth?

A new book was about to tell them.

## ✧ 7 ✧

# Can It Be True?

*What are flying saucers?*
*Where do they come from?*
*How do they fly?*
*Have they been found on earth?*

*These questions . . . are discussed in this believe-it-or-not book—a story stranger than fiction which may prove that journeys through space are as commonplace as an ordinary milk-run.*

These were the words printed on the dust jacket of *Behind the Flying Saucers*, a book that picked up where Mr. X's lecture had left off. Its author, Frank Scully, claimed his was the "true" story of flying saucers and that "scientists and other experts in such fields as magnetic energy, astronomy, and aerodynamics—men who are reputedly high in their profession but whose names must be kept anonymous," had revealed the information to him.

Those anonymous men were Mr. X and Dr. Gee.

And the book's revelations went on for two hundred fifty pages.

Drawing from the Aztec, New Mexico, story, Scully described the alien beings as humanoids, about three feet tall, green, and from Venus. As in Scientist X's lecture, their spaceships were powered by magnetism and made of a mysterious metal far harder than anything found on Earth. But the author also added his own embellishments—lots of them, like:

- All saucers' dimensions were divisible by nine.
- Venusian used a pictorial-style kind of writing, similar to Egyptian hieroglyphs. A booklet of extraterrestrial script had been found in the wreckage, but scientists still couldn't translate it.

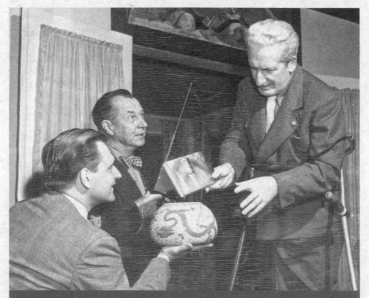

Frank Scully (standing) uses a copy of his book *Behind the Flying Saucers* to demonstrate to Dr. X (center) the orbit of the earth and its magnetic fields. The bowl is held by radio salesman George Koehler.

- The extraterrestrial crew wore blue space suits made of a fabric that did not tear.
- They carried watches that ran on the "magnetic day," which was twenty-three hours and fifty-eight minutes long.
- Their teeth were perfect—no cavities.
- Venusian food came in the form of nutrient-packed wafers.

- Flying saucers didn't have bathrooms. Since a trip from Venus to Earth took just minutes, they didn't need them. Apparently, Venusians could hold it that long.

But the book's central premise was this: Flying saucers had crashed on Earth, and both the saucers and the dead crew had been secreted away by the United States government. Authorities hadn't told the public because they feared widespread panic. The military was convinced that if Americans knew the truth, there would be pandemonium.

Scully had no evidence to back up any of his claims. Completely undocumented, the book was based almost entirely on the word of Mr. X and Dr. Gee. Nothing more. Had Dr. Broman's science students evaluated the book, they would certainly have concluded it was baloney.

None of that mattered to book buyers. Published in the waning days of summer 1950, *Behind the Flying Saucers* quickly landed on the *New York Times*

Nonfiction Bestseller List. It remained there for the next seventeen weeks.

Written in an informal style, the book was easy to read. Unfortunately, in 1950, few readers were scientifically literate enough to know that the book's pages brimmed with technical-sounding nonsense. Scully had scrambled scientific concepts and distorted facts. Hundreds of scientists and engineers called out the book as "laughable" and nothing but "scientific gobbledygook." But ordinary readers devoured every word. They began to identify alien beings with the qualities and traits described in Scully's book. Soon, it was generally accepted that extraterrestrials were short, green, and humanoid; possessed advanced technology; and arrived in flying saucers that could perform maneuvers impossible for human-made aircraft. Additionally, these saucers were fast, made of material not found on Earth, and powered by a mysterious source.

*Behind the Flying Saucers* left another indelible mark, too. In the American imagination, crashed saucers and government cover-ups were now forever linked.

## ✧ 8 ✧

# Who Are These Mysterious Little Men?

Everything was going great for Frank Scully. He'd made money. He'd gained fame as a flying saucer expert. And some people were even calling him a hero for exposing the truth about the government's UFO cover-up. Then the September 1952 issue of *True* magazine hit newsstands. It featured an article by reporter J. P. Cahn titled "The Flying Saucers and the Mysterious Little Men," chronicling Cahn's hunt for the truth about Scully's book. "For four months and across 4,500 miles I tracked down visitors from the planet Venus," Cahn wrote. "And although I didn't find the dead Venusians, I uncovered some rather fantastic living creatures."

One of those "creatures" was Mr. X. Cahn discovered his real name was Silas Newton. And old newspaper files revealed Newton to be a con artist. Not only had Newton been arrested and charged with selling worthless stock, but he'd also bilked a Texas oil company out of thousands of dollars with a fake invention he claimed could locate oil. No wonder Newton preferred the anonymity of "Mr. X."

Cahn also tracked down Dr. Gee who—according to Scully's book—had "headed up 1,700 scientists doing 35,000 experiments on land, in the sea and air, and spending one billion dollars in a top secret government magnetic research project." Dr. Gee sounded like an eminent scientist. The truth? Dr. Gee didn't exist. It was an alias for Leo GeBauer, the owner of a television and radio parts store in Phoenix, Arizona.

As for the flying saucer's indestructible extraterrestrial material, Cahn managed to get his hands on the sample that Newton, posing as Mr. X, had shown to the science students. The reporter sent it to the Stanford Institute for testing. The results came back conclusive. The sample was nothing more than a common aluminum alloy used for making pots and pans. The researchers easily melted down the "indestructible" material to a puddle of silver-colored liquid.

Did Frank Scully know any of this? Cahn didn't believe so. "I learned that two men—Silas Newton and Leo GeBauer—had manufactured the hoax and fobbed it off on a gullible author." Why had they done it? Cahn thought he knew, but he couldn't prove his suspicions. "And what you can't prove, you don't print," he wrote.

It was a lesson Frank Scully obviously hadn't learned.

# ✧ 9 ✧

## Saucers over the White House?

Just before midnight on July 19, 1952, air traffic controller Edward Nugent at Washington, DC's National Airport spotted seven slow-moving objects on his radar screen. He called over his supervisor. "Here's a fleet of flying saucers for you," he joked. At the same time, two more air traffic controllers spied a strange bright light in the distance that suddenly zipped away at incredible speed.

At nearby Andrews Air Force Base, radar operators were seeing the same unidentified blips. They started out slow and clustered, then raced away at speeds exceeding 7,000 miles per hour. Looking out

An airman peers at his radar scope.

his window, one Andrews' controller saw what he described as "an orange ball of fire trailing a tail."

Around the same time, a commercial pilot flying over Washington, DC, could not believe his eyes. He reported seeing six streaking bright lights, "like falling stars without tails."

Back at National Airport, controllers had stopped making flying saucer jokes. The objects buzzed past the Capitol Building and above the White

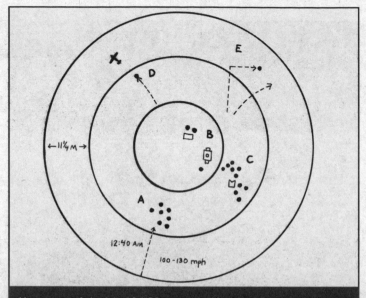

Maneuvers of the July 19 UFOs over Washington, DC, can be traced on this diagram of a radar scope. At (A) seven objects approach the nation's capital from the south. At (B) some are seen over the White House and Capitol. At (C) they appear over Andrews Air Force Base. At (D) one tracks an airliner. At (E) one is seen to make a sharp right-angle turn.

House. Was this some sort of attack? The Air Force quickly scrambled two F-94C jets to intercept the objects.

In the air, the pilots spied the objects. They locked on with their radar. And then? To the bewilderment of both pilots and air traffic controllers, the UFOs disappeared.

An F-94C like the kind that chased after the UFOs.

It went on this way for hours: the objects appeared, the jets gave chase, and the objects vanished. The UFOs' behavior led some air traffic controllers to wonder if the mysterious crafts could intercept and understand radio traffic. What *were* those things?

At last, as the sun rose over the Capitol Building, the objects disappeared—this time for good.

But the very next Saturday, they were back. Two more F-94Cs gave chase. Once again, the jets soared to a location, only for the objects to disappear.

# SAUCERS OVER WASHINGTON, D.C.

HARRY G. BARNES, SENIOR AIR ROUTE TRAFFIC CONTROLLER FOR THE CIVIL AERONAUTICS ADMINISTRATION, WAS IN CHARGE OF THE NATIONAL AIRPORT, WASHINGTON, D.C., A.R.T. CONTROL CENTER ON THE NIGHT OF JULY 19, 1952. "BRIEFY," HE STATES IN A NEWSPAPER ARTICLE, "...OUR JOB IS TO CONSTANTLY MONITOR THE SKIES AROUND THE NATION'S CAPITOL WITH THE ELECTRONIC EYE OF RADAR..." SHORTLY AFTER MIDNIGHT ON THAT DATE, SEVEN PIPS APPEARED SUDDENLY ON THE CONTROL CENTER'S SCOPE. ED NUGENT, JIM COPELAND, AND JIM RITCHEY, ALL EXPERIENCED RADAR CONTROLLERS, CHECKED THE OBSERVATIONS. THE AIRPORT CONTROL TOWER RADAR OPERATOR VERIFIED THE SAME SIGHTING. *THEY WERE OVER "THE RESTRICTED AREAS OF WASHINGTON, INCLUDING THE WHITE HOUSE AND THE CAPITOL..."*

CAPTAIN C.S. PIERMAN, A CAPITOL AIRLINES PILOT OF 17 YEARS FLYING EXPERIENCE, SHORTLY AFTER TAKING OFF, WAS ASKED TO CHECK THESE MYSTERIOUS OBJECTS. HE RADIOED BACK...

*THERE'S ONE... AND THERE IT GOES!*

PIERMAN DESCRIBED IT AS A BRIGHT LIGHT MOVING FASTER, AT TIMES, THAN A SHOOTING STAR...

BARNES STATES: "DURING THE NEXT 14 MINUTES, HE (PIERMAN) REPORTED THAT HE SAW SIX SUCH LIGHTS... *EACH SIGHTING COINCIDED WITH A PIP WE COULD SEE NEAR HIS PLANE.* WHEN *HE* REPORTED THAT THE LIGHT *STREAKED OFF AT HIGH SPEED,* IT *DISAPPEARED* FROM *OUR SCOPE...*"

THAT MEANS IT ZOOMED OUT OF OUR BEAM *BETWEEN SWEEPS!* IT *ACCELERATED* FROM *130* MILES PER HOUR TO ALMOST *500* IN LESS THAN *4 SECONDS...*

This comic book, created weeks after the events of July 19, 1952, dramatically detailed what became known to the Air Force as "the big flap." While it read like science fiction, it was completely true.

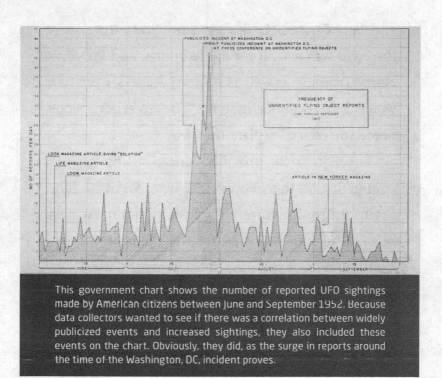

FREQUENCY OF
UNIDENTIFIED FLYING OBJECT REPORTS
JUNE THROUGH SEPTEMBER
1952

This government chart shows the number of reported UFO sightings made by American citizens between June and September 1952. Because data collectors wanted to see if there was a correlation between widely publicized events and increased sightings, they also included these events on the chart. Obviously, they did, as the surge in reports around the time of the Washington, DC, incident proves.

Finally, one of the pilots caught sight of a bright light in the distance. He raced after it. "I was at my maximum speed," the pilot later reported, "but . . . I ceased chasing them because I saw no chance of overtaking them."

The next morning, newspaper headlines across the country screamed, "Saucers Swarm Over Capital," and "Jets Chase D.C. Sky Ghosts." Press coverage of the event was reaching a fevered pitch, and President Harry Truman, as well as military leaders, worried it would lead to public hysteria. The American people needed an official explanation *now*.

The Air Force provided one. Calling a press conference at the Pentagon, Major General John Stamford told reporters that the pilots must have seen stars or meteors. As for the radar anomalies, this could be explained by a temperature inversion over the city, making it nothing more than a weather-related event.

This explanation satisfied the press.

It satisfied most Americans, too.

But it didn't satisfy Air Force Captain Ed Ruppelt. He returned to his Dayton, Ohio, office stumped—maybe it *had* been spaceships.

# ✧ 10 ✧

## Does the Air Force Believe in UFOs . . . or Doesn't It?

With its standard-issue military furniture and stacks of brown folder files, the office at Wright-Patterson Air Force Base in Dayton, Ohio, hardly looked like the headquarters of a highly classified project.

And the two men who shared the office certainly looked ordinary. There was twenty-nine-year-old Captain Ed Ruppelt, the chief of the project, who'd popularized the phrase "unidentified flying objects," because so many of them didn't look like flying saucers. And there was Dr. J. Allen Hynek, an astronomer from the Department of Physics and

Captain Ed Ruppelt in 1955.

Astronomy at the University of Ohio who'd been hired by the Air Force as a scientific consultant.

Together, they were on a covert mission: to track down and investigate UFO sightings for the US Air Force.

In truth, the Air Force had been quietly looking into flying saucers for years (all the while downplaying them to the American public). But in 1952, as

Dr. J. Allen Hynek at a press conference in 1966 debunking a so-called photograph of a flying saucer.

waves of sightings from around the nation continued, the Air Force intensified its efforts. It opened up a behind-the-scenes UFO organization with no public oversight called Project Blue Book.

Blue Book's assignment wasn't to unravel the mysteries of UFOs. Air Force generals didn't care whether an object came from some country on Earth, or some distant solar system. They just needed to know if it was dangerous. Did it pose a risk to national security? Blue Book's job was to answer that question.

The first page of Project Blue Book's Status Report for 1952, in which investigators summarized for higher-ups the cases they'd looked into for that year.

It did its work under top secret protocols. Observation posts were set up on air bases around the country, and air-traffic controllers were secretly given 35-millimeter cameras to film anything unusual. Meanwhile, data-collection officers met with hundreds of citizens. They developed a special procedure for questioning those who claimed to see UFOs. First, the witness was asked to "draw a picture that will show the shape of the object." Next came a series of questions: "What was the condition of the sky? Did the object suddenly speed up or rush away at any time? Did it change shape? Flicker, throb or pulsate?" After gathering all the information, officials asked witnesses "out of patriotic duty" not to whisper a word about the interview. Incredibly, most stayed silent.

If Blue Book investigators proved that a UFO sighting was not a national security threat, then they looked for other explanations. Dr. Hynek, who'd joined the project believing that UFOs were "just a lot of nonsense," was especially good at finding logical reasons for strange occurrences. He blamed them on mirages, gases, flocks of birds, and "figments of the imagination," among other things. "I enjoyed the role of debunker," Hynek wrote later,

The first page of Project Blue Book's questionnaire given to people claiming to have seen a UFO.

"even though I had to admit that some of the ... cases *were* real puzzlers."

In the seventeen years Project Blue Book operated, agents investigated 12,618 cases. Almost all were explained away. But 701 defied explanation. They were, indeed, puzzlers.

In July 1952, a US Coast Guard photographer snapped this picture at the Salem, Massachusetts, air station that shows unidentified objects flying in a V-formation. Blue Book investigators explained away these UFOs as a meteorological event.

Take, for example, the Lubbock Lights of August 25, 1951, when three earth science professors spotted a crescent of some two dozen lights flashing silently across the west Texas sky. A few nights later, a college student took photos of them, showing,

This photo, purportedly of a flying saucer, was taken on November 23, 1951, in Riverside, California. The unidentified photographer told reporters he'd snapped the picture as the "thing" flew past him for a second time. Project Blue Book, however, determined the photo was a fake. The saucer was actually an automobile hubcap thrown into the air and photographed.

in several exposures, a large luminous blob, "like a mother craft hovering near its aerial brood." The earth scientists calculated the objects' top speed at 18,000 miles an hour. The Air Force, after

In 1952, a New York City man took this picture from the roof of his apartment building. Notice the oblong object directly beneath the moon. Project Blue Book investigators could not explain this UFO. In their records, they marked it as "unknown."

examining the student's photographs, declared them genuine. So what was it? No one knew.

Or what about the sighting by prominent astronomer Clyde Tombaugh, the discoverer of Pluto? On a summer's night in 1948, he was sitting in his backyard in Las Cruces, New Mexico, with his wife and mother-in-law when they saw something glide overhead. They all agreed it was a "ship" of some kind, oval shaped and glowing green blue. It flew so low they could see a half-dozen windows along the side of the craft. Air Force investigators noted that the Tombaughs' description of the ship bore a close resemblance to a sighting reported by two pilots in the area. Both groups of witnesses said it flew too fast for a plane, and two slow for a meteor. Both insisted it was not like any aircraft on Earth. What was it? No one knew.

And then there was the flaming ball spotted in January 1952 by the tail gunner and another crew-member of a B-29 on a solo flight over Korea. About the size of a beach ball, the orange object pulsed, and had a halo of bluish flame. For five minutes it followed the B-29. Then it pulled ahead and shot away. On the same night, eighty miles away, another B-29 crew spotted a similar flaming ball. What was it? No one knew.

Hynek's attitude toward UFOs began to change. These cases had multiple, reliable witnesses. Many had physical evidence—radar data, photographs, marks on the ground, or on airplanes. What did he make of that? These sightings, he came to believe, demanded far more scientific attention than Blue Book gave them. He knew he would never get the Air Force to change its mind about the purpose of the project. That would be, he said, like "fighting City Hall." Still, he was beginning to feel that the "UFO phenomena is real and that efforts to investigate it and solve it, could have a profound effect . . . [on] man's view of himself and his place in the universe."

Of course, Dr. Hynek didn't say this in public . . . not yet.

Meanwhile, Project Blue Book continued secretly collecting and dismissing reports of flying saucers, spheres, and crescents; green fireballs and bright, white lights; V-shaped ships, floating cigars, extraterrestrials—dead *and* alive.

# ✦ 11 ✦

## Who Is Watching the Skies?

Laura Marxer's head spun with flying saucers. Where had they come from? What lurked inside? She wondered. She worried. She burned to know. That's why she formed the Flying Saucer Club of Detroit in August 1954. She hoped to discover the answers through debate and discussion. To her surprise, dozens of people joined. They came from all walks of life—farmers, doctors, factory workers, teachers, retirees, and students. But they all had one thing in common: an obsession with flying saucers and visitors from other worlds. Now, on the second Tuesday of every month, Laura grabbed her notebook—the one she'd covered with drawings of spaceships—and headed over to the community room in Detroit's civic center. There, club members imbibed both refreshments and "saucerian conversation," as Laura called it.

Hers wasn't the only flying saucer club. Throughout the 1950s, hundreds of groups just like Laura's popped up across the country. UFO obsessives met in public spaces like church basements and school gymnasiums. They traded newspaper and magazine articles about UFO sightings. They debated possibilities and wrestled to make sense of what was in the skies.

There was urgency and seriousness to these clubs. Members didn't believe what the government was telling them about UFOs, and so they felt compelled to do their own investigating. Many even believed the government was watching them. And, in truth, they were right. The government *was* watching! Saucer clubs often published newsletters in which they detailed their findings and theories, as well as chronicled any new UFO sightings. Both Project Blue Book and the CIA monitored these newsletters. They weren't just keeping an eye out for UFO information. They were also making sure members hadn't uncovered any military secrets during their saucer investigations.

Meanwhile, American's paranoia continued to grow. Their fear of nuclear annihilation manifested itself in anxieties about interplanetary attack. And popular movies of the 1950s—*The Thing From Another World* (1951), *The War of the Worlds* (1953), *Invasion of the Body Snatchers* (1956), and dozens more—capitalized on and further spread these anxieties.

Was it any wonder memberships in saucer clubs grew . . . and grew . . . and grew? Soon, local clubs joined with other local clubs. These eventually expanded into statewide UFO clubs with names like the Civilian Saucer Investigations Organization of California, which naturally grew into even larger national organizations. Conferences began to be held in cities around the country. Hundreds, even thousands of UFO enthusiasts gathered at these events to debate, speculate, and theorize. They crammed lecture halls to hear the leading UFO

A poster from the 1956 movie *Earth vs. the Flying Saucers* depicts many Americans' biggest fear: attack from overhead and warnings to "take cover."

hunters of the day—now called ufologists—speak about extraterrestrial encounters.

"Keep watching the skies," urged Donald Keyhoe, the foremost ufologist of the 1950s. Keyhoe, a Naval Academy graduate and decorated combat aviator, believed flying saucers were real, and posed a dire threat. Alien beings had been watching Earth, he declared, ever since humankind had unlocked the fearsome secrets of the atomic

An actor, dressed as an extraterrestrial, promotes the 1951 science fiction movie *The Man From Planet X*. Ads for the movie declared that extraterrestrial invasion "is closer than you think."

bomb. They could land at any moment. And the US government knew it. It was time for officials to come clean about UFOs. The American people could take the truth. "We have survived the stunning impact of the Atomic Age," he said. "We should be able to take the Interplanetary Age, when it comes, without hysteria."

In 1956, he cofounded the National Investigations Committee on Aerial Phenomena (NICAP) to counter the Air Force's public position that UFOs were nonsense. Keyhoe frequently appeared on TV and radio programs in which he ranted about the government's deep and secret involvement with UFOs. Not only was the Air Force covering up information, he insisted, but so was the CIA. "Will no one tell us the truth?" he repeatedly raged. "There is an urgent need to know." His fiery remarks added to a growing sense of public distrust in government.

NICAP quickly grew into the biggest and most prominent civilian UFO research group in the country. The group pestered the Air Force for its files, and it called for Congressional hearings to acknowledge the reality of the "saucer problem." Additionally, Keyhoe pressed for the creation of a government program dedicated to finding a way to communicate

COMMONLY REPORTED UFO TYPES

Note: These drawings are hypothetical constructions, generalized from hundreds of UFO reports. They are intended to indicate basic shapes which have been reported, and are not necessarily completely accurate in every detail. Additional details sometimes reported, such as "portholes," projections, body lights, etc., are not portrayed. The general types shown do represent with reasonable accuracy virtually all UFOs which have been reliably described in any detail. Examples of each type appear in the left-hand column.

| UFO SHAPE | BOTTOM VIEW | BOTTOM ANGLE | SIDE VIEW |
|---|---|---|---|

1. FLAT DISC
A. 10-54 Cox
   7-2-52 Newhouse
B. 7-9-47 Johnson
   7-14-52 Nash

A B (Bottom Angle) — oval
A "lens-shaped" B "coin-like" (Side View)

2. DOMED DISC
A. 9-21-58 Fitzgerald
   4-24-62 Gasslein
B. 5-11-50 Trent
   8-7-52 Jansen

A B (Bottom Angle) — "hat-shaped"
A "World War I helmet" B (Side View)

3. SATURN DISC (Double dome)
A. 10-4-54 Salandin
   1-16-58 Trindade
   10-2-61 Harris
B. 8-20-56 Moore

A
B
elliptical or "winged oval" — "diamond-shaped" — "Saturn-shaped"

4. HEMISPHERICAL DISC
9-24-59 Redmond
1-21-61 Pulliam
2-7-61 Walley

"parachute" — "mushroom" "half moon"

5. FLATTENED SPHERE
10-1-48 Gorman
4-27-50 Adickes
10-9-51 C.A.A.

sometimes with peak

6. SPHERICAL (Circular from all angles)
3-45 Delarof
1-20-52 Baller
10-12-61 Edwards

A
metallic-appearing ball
B — ball of glowing light

7. ELLIPTICAL
12-20-58 Arboreen
11-2-57 Levelland
8-13-60 Carson

"football" "egg-shaped"

8. TRIANGULAR
5-7-56 G.O.C.
5-22-60 Majorca

"tear-drop"

9. CYLINDRICAL (Rocket-like)
8-1-46 Puckett
7-23-48 Chiles

"cigar-shaped"

10. LIGHT SOURCE ONLY
"star-like" or "planet-like"

What shape is your UFO? A 1964 NICAP publication titled "The UFO Evidence" included this chart of commonly reported unidentified flying object types for easy identification.

with the alien beings. "Extraterrestrials" he said, "must be convinced that humans will not invade other worlds." In case communication failed, he called on the military to prepare a defense program against extraterrestrial invasion.

The government ignored Keyhoe and NICAP. In the privacy of the Project Blue Book office, Captain Ruppelt called Keyhoe a "saucer screwball." The ufologist, he said, was like a "hypochondriac at the doctor's; nothing will make him believe the diagnosis unless it is what he came to hear . . . [Sadly] there are plenty of saucer screwballs." Added another Blue Book agent, "It isn't the UFOs that give us trouble; it's the people."

Other national UFO groups cropped up, too, most notably Ground Saucer Watch. Established by scientists and engineers, it used scientific criteria to resolve controversial sightings. It also issued press releases and sponsored lectures. But perhaps most importantly, the group pursued legal action, suing the federal government for release of its UFO material. Did the government suppress reports of

THE
HYNEK
UFO
REPORT

Dr. J. ALLEN HYNEK
AUTHOR OF
THE UFO EXPERIENCE

THE
LATEST
BESTSELLER
BY THE WORLD'S
LEADING UFO
EXPERT

Dr. Hynek began writing popular books like this one about the more puzzling facts of UFOs. In these books, he chronicled for the public those cases he called "puzzlers" and encouraged further scientific study of them.

the sightings in the press? Did it muzzle witnesses? Did it withhold files and hide information? Saucer Watch demanded answers.

It would be decades before they got any.

In the intervening years, more ufology groups emerged, including Citizens Against UFO Secrecy, the Mutual UFO Network, and the Aerial Phenomena Research Organization.

And at Northwestern University in Evanston, Illinois, former Blue Book investigator, Dr. J. Allen Hynek, established his Center for UFO Studies. Restricted to scientists and other experts, Hynek's organization dedicated itself to rigorous investigation and serious study of interplanetary travel. Hynek even established an archive of UFO documents, reports, and materials—the first of its kind.

The debunker had become a believer. "Certainly, a careful study of the more extraordinary UFO cases . . . leaves little doubt that an 'intelligence' of some sort is operating," he wrote. "But what kind and where from?"

## ✦ 12 ✦

## Close Encounters or Wacky Stories?

In Roswell, the events of 1947 had not been forgotten. They weren't spoken about publicly, but there were whispers. As the memories of those involved grew faulty, rumors swirled. So did speculation and exaggerations. Witnesses died. Facts got confused. The truth grew blurry.

Time passed.

In 1967, the Air Force base near Roswell closed. So did the White Sands Proving Ground and the Los Alamos Laboratory. It was said that the military now built and tested its classified weapons at a top secret facility in Nevada called Area 51.

In 1969, astronauts landed on the moon, proving that space travel *was* possible. Six months later, the Air Force shut down Project Blue Book. After seventeen years of investigating sightings, it had at last determined that UFOs posed no threat to security.

In 1974, President Richard Nixon resigned after breaking the law, then trying to cover it up. The effect on public trust was dramatic. That year, polls

A poster created in the 1960s by the United States Information Service to promote the nation's achievements in space exploration.

View from the presidential helicopter of Richard Nixon (right) as he leaves the White House for the final time on the day of his resignation, August 9, 1974. As Vice President Gerald Ford (left) looks on, Patricia Nixon kisses Betty Ford goodbye. Behind are Nixon's daughters and sons-in-law.

showed just one in three Americans trusted the government. Authorities lied, they now believed, and conspiracies were commonplace.

In 1975, the military declassified Project Blue Book's records. Now the public could see exactly what the Air Force had been up to all those years. And ufologists could delve into decades-old case files.

In 1977, Americans flocked to see Steven Spielberg's *Close Encounters of the Third Kind* (its title taken from a phrase coined by Dr. Hynek, who even had a bit part in the movie). They thronged theaters to see *Star Wars*. Enormous hits, these movies reignited American's fascination with outer space and extraterrestrials. So did the remake of *Invasion of the Body Snatchers* (1979) and *E.T. The Extra-Terrestrial* (1982).

Television, too, served up a galaxy of space shows, including *The Lost Saucer* (1975), *Mork and Mindy* (1978), *Battlestar Galactica* (1978), and *Project U.F.O.* (1978), with its episodes ripped from the case files of Project Blue Book.

Was it any wonder that a new crop of sensational UFO stories appeared in the media? They included

CLOSE ENCOUNTER
OF THE FIRST KIND
Sighting of a UFO

CLOSE ENCOUNTER
OF THE SECOND KIND
Physical Evidence

CLOSE ENCOUNTER
OF THE THIRD KIND
Contact

CLOSE ENCOUNTERS
OF THE THIRD KIND

The movie poster for *Close Encounters of the Third Kind.* Note the definitions of the three kinds of UFO encounters. These are Dr. Hynek's classifications, based on his years of data gathering at Project Blue Book.

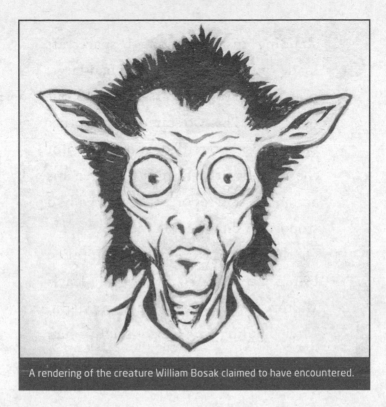

A rendering of the creature William Bosak claimed to have encountered.

strange claims of encounters with alien beings like these:

- As Wisconsin dairy farmer William Bosak drove home on a foggy night in December 1974, he noticed something on the side of the road. He slowed for a look. It was a ten-foot-tall humanoid standing inside a domed spacecraft made of glass. The creature had large, protruding eyes and ears that stuck out of its head. The two stared at each other before Bosak, terrified, sped away. But the next day the farmer regretted his action. He told reporters he wished he'd stopped to show he was friendly.

- On the night of November 5, 1975, alien beings zapped Arizona logger Travis Walton with a bright beam of light. After hauling the unconscious man aboard their spaceship, they flew him around the universe. Five days later, they dropped him off on the side of a deserted road.

- While on patrol duty in the early morning hours of August 27, 1979, Marshal County (Minnesota) Sheriff's Deputy Van Johnson hit a UFO—a brilliant, white light floating four feet above the road. The impact smashed the car's windshield and sent it spinning into a ditch. Incredibly, Johnson wasn't hurt. But ever after, both his wristwatch and the clock on the car's dash mysteriously ticked fourteen minutes slow.

Ufologists, meanwhile, were having a field day. Not all of them, however, chose to investigate these recent claims. Stanton Friedman, a nuclear physicist-turned-UFO-researcher, had been reexamining old UFO reports. Most of these had been declared "solved" by the Air Force. But were they really? One case in particular fascinated Friedman. It involved mysterious debris found on a ranch outside Roswell, New Mexico. The Air Force claimed the stuff came from a weather balloon. Friedman didn't buy it.

He started digging, and soon became convinced that something *big* had happened in the New Mexican desert in the summer of 1947.

Something dark and secret.

Something of earthshaking importance.

But would anyone talk to him about it?

# PART 3

## It Crashed at Roswell . . . Right?

## ✧ 13 ✧

## Did You *Personally* See a Crashed Flying Saucer?

On an overcast day in 1978, Stanton Friedman and his research partner, Bill Moore, drove into Roswell and started asking questions. "[We] went after the story the hard way," Friedman later admitted. "There was no Internet back then. We went to the libraries, dug through telephone records, made call after call."

Mack Brazel had died in 1969. So had Sheriff George Wilcox. The case was cold. And then . . . a tip! Major Jesse Marcel—the intelligence officer and first member of the military to examine the debris—was alive and well in Louisiana. Friedman and Moore rushed to talk with him. They asked the most important question first.

"Major Marcel, did you personally see a crashed UFO?"

Marcel, now a gray-haired grandfather, shook his head. "I saw a lot of wreckage, but no machine," he replied. He thought it possible that "whatever it was" had exploded in the air, scattering debris over Mack Brazel's pasture before crashing to the earth some distance to the west.

Marcel, however, couldn't verify this theory. He hadn't heard about it through Air Force channels, and that made sense. "If another military group had become involved with a larger piece of wreckage, there would be no reason for me to be informed about it, officially."

Moore now asked Marcel what he thought when he first saw the debris. Was it a weather balloon?

"It was not," replied Marcel firmly. "I was pretty well acquainted with most everything that was in the air at the time, both ours and foreign . . . It was definitely not a weather or tracking device, nor was it a plane or a missile . . . It was something I had never seen before."

He and Cavitt had collected all the debris. There was a lot of the stuff, he said. The men filled the back of a pickup truck, as well as the trunk and back seat of a four-door Buick sedan. The next afternoon, July 8, military staff loaded it all onto a B-29. There was so much of it that it filled half the plane.

Friedman was surprised. Half a plane's worth? That was far more debris than had been originally reported, wasn't it? The ufologist riffled through his notes. Yes, here it was: In 1947, Marcel had indicated that the debris field was smaller than he'd expected, and that most of the stuff had been picked up either by the Brazel family, or by himself and Cavitt. So why was Marcel changing his story? Friedman thought he knew. Marcel had been part of the government's cover-up. He couldn't tell the truth back then. But he was telling it now.

What happened next?

Marcel accompanied the wreckage to the base in Fort Worth.

"[I] was told to bring some of the stuff up to [General Ramey's] office . . . We did this and spread it out on the floor on some brown paper . . . It was only a very small portion of the debris." General Ramey then invited the press to take pictures. They even took a few shots of Marcel holding the "less-interesting metallic debris." The press wasn't allowed to get close to the stuff. They weren't allowed to touch it. After a few minutes, staff shooed reporters out of the room and cleared away the debris.

And then?

They substituted the Roswell wreckage with some of their own, said Marcel. This debris—the replacement stuff—really was from a weather balloon. "Then they allowed more photos," said Marcel. The general and one of his aides posed in these pictures. By that time, "the actual wreckage was already on its way to Wright Field [in Ohio]."

Friedman and Moore felt exhilarated. Here was proof—an eyewitness—claiming the Air Force had intentionally fooled the press. "So you're saying this whole weather balloon thing was nothing but a cover-up," pressed Friedman.

Marcel didn't say yes. But he didn't say no either. Instead, he replied, "One thing that I want to point out is that newspapers saw very little of the material—and none of the important things that had hieroglyphics, or markings on them. They didn't see that because it wasn't there . . ." In other words, the Air Force had purposely not shown it to them.

Marcel looked Friedman in the eyes. "I repeat, the material I saw came from no weather balloon."

But the major never called it a flying saucer either. And he never claimed to see extraterrestrials dead, or alive.

Those details came from another source.

Vern and Jean Maltais, a married couple in their mid-sixties, couldn't wait to share their story. Well . . . actually it wasn't *their* story. The things they were about to tell Friedman and Moore had not happened to *them*. They'd happened to their good friend

A model of the flying saucer purported to have been seen by Barney Bjarnett.

Barney Barnett, who'd worked as a civil engineer for the federal government. Barnett, they went on, had told them the story in 1950. Yes, thirty years had passed since then. Still, they remembered every word he'd said. But they'd never repeated it . . . until now.

On the morning of July 3, 1947, Barnett had been working out in the desert when something bright and metallic glinted in the distance, Vern told the ufologists. Curious, he set off to see what it was. He walked about a mile. Then he saw it—a disc-shaped object made of metal, about twenty-five or thirty feet across. Barnett stood there, gaping and disbelieving. Was he truly seeing a flying saucer?

Just then, a group of people came up from the opposite direction. They told Barnett they were an archaeological research team from the University of Pennsylvania. They'd been digging in the area when they, too, had seen metallic glinting. Thinking it was a plane crash, they'd gone in search of it.

Together, Barnett and the archaeologists walked around to the back of the saucer. They stopped. Dead bodies. Obviously, they'd been thrown from the wreck. Barnett thought there were probably more bodies inside.

"They were like human, but not human," Vern Maltais recalled Barnett telling him. "The heads were round, the eyes were small and they had no hair . . . Their clothing seemed to be one-piece and gray in color. You couldn't see any zipper, belts, or buttons. They seemed to be all males . . ."

What happened next, asked Friedman.

A military truck arrived, followed shortly by other army personnel. They quickly cordoned off the area. An official ordered Barnett and the others to leave immediately. He told them it was their patriotic duty to remain quiet about what they'd seen.

Jean Maltais spoke up. Her husband had told it exactly right. That was just what Barnett had said so long ago. Now, she added a detail. Barnett had watched the army take the saucer away in a big truck. They took the bodies away, too.

Did the couple remember where this crash site had been?

"No, I don't exactly recall," replied Jean Maltais. "I remember he said it was the prairie—'the Flats' is the way he put it."

Friedman wondered. Could Barnett have meant the Plains of San Agustin, also called locally, "the Flats?" That was two hundred miles from Roswell. He thought back to the interview with Major

Marcel. Marcel had theorized that a damaged flying saucer had scattered debris over Brazel's ranch before crashing someplace else. Could this have happened? Could the debris have come from the saucer Barnett saw? Freidman felt certain the events were linked. They were too extraordinary not to be.

Too bad he and Moore couldn't verify the story by speaking with Barney Barnett. Unfortunately, he'd died years earlier. The Maltaises, however, assured them that Barnett would never have fabricated such a story. He'd been an upstanding citizen. A few phone calls made by Friedman to others who'd known Barnett verified this. The civil engineer *had* been a good guy. And that was enough for Friedman and Moore. They believed the couple's story—every word.

But should they have? The Maltaises weren't witnesses to the event. They hadn't seen anything themselves. They'd merely repeated what someone else had said—someone who could no longer be asked about it. Had Barnett lied to his friends so long ago? For that matter, how did the ufologists know the Maltaises weren't lying now? In a courtroom, the couple's testimony would be called "hearsay" and wouldn't be allowed as evidence. Of course, this wasn't a court case. But didn't the Maltaises' claim require more evidence? According to longtime UFO researchers Tom Carey and Donald Schmitt, valid investigations into extraterrestrial encounters required a "search for incriminating, physical evidence [photographs, artifacts, documents, fingerprints, DNA traces] . . . coupled with relevant and credible eyewitness testimony."

Vern and Jean Maltais were not providing "eyewitness testimony." Did it matter?

Doggedly, Friedman searched for a connection between Barnett's crashed flying saucer and the debris found on the Brazel ranch. He found it on the front page of the *Roswell Daily Record* for Tuesday, July 8, 1947, beneath the headline "Roswell Hardware Man and Wife Report Disk Seen." As he read the decades-old newspaper account, Friedman grew more and more excited.

As Roswell resident Dan Wilmot had told reporters back then, he'd been sitting on the front porch of his Roswell home when "all of a sudden, a big glowing object zoomed out of the sky . . . at a high rate of speed." Startled, he and his wife, Mary Grace, had dashed out into the front yard. They looked up. Passing directly overhead was an oval-shaped object, glowing as if lit from inside. It made a "slight swishing sound," as it glided past.

All this had occurred, "at about ten minutes to ten on the evening of July 2, 1947." But neither Wilmot nor his wife reported the sighting or spoke to anyone about it. They didn't want folks in town to make fun of them. But then, on July 8, the army base put out their press release about finding a flying disc, and they felt safe sharing their story. That same day, Dan and Mary Grace hurried down to the newspaper office, where they told reporters everything. Their story appeared on the front page the next morning alongside a banner headline that read "RAAF Captures Flying Saucer on Ranch In Roswell Region."

The ufologist took the Wilmots' story at face value, too. After all, the article in the *Roswell Daily Record* described Dan Wilmot as "one of the most respected and reliable citizens in town." And reliable citizens never lied or exaggerated, did they?

Friedman pored over his notes. The Wilmots' story jibed with that of the Maltaises. Wilmot and his wife had seen a UFO overhead on July 2. The next day— July 3—Barney Barnett had found a crashed saucer. Obviously, they'd all seen the same spacecraft. But how did their accounts fit with Mack Brazel's version of events? They didn't. During an interview with the press on July 8, 1947, Brazel said he'd found the debris three weeks earlier, in mid-June. But that didn't make sense. Struggling to understand the connection, Friedman pondered various possibilities. He recalled what Major Jesse Marcel had said about the debris coming from a damaged saucer, as well as his claims of government cover-up.

He began putting the pieces together. They didn't quite fit.

So Friedman and Moore conducted more interviews. They talked with Mack Brazel's daughter, Bessie, as well as his former neighbors, Floyd and Loretta Proctor. All three remembered the pressure placed on Brazel by the military. Floyd Proctor even claimed they'd kept the rancher "at the base for about a week under guard. He was real talkative about that [debris] until he came back; then he wouldn't say much at all."

Friedman took Bessie and the Proctors at their words. The ufologist now believed he knew what happened: Brazel had lied to the press. The government had forced him to say he'd found the wreckage in mid-June when he'd actually found it on July 3. It was all part of a vast cover-up.

He couldn't prove this was true. He and Moore hadn't found any solid evidence. There were no records of Brazel being arrested or detained by authorities. Additionally, no one knew with certainty when Brazel had first found the debris. Friedman's theory was based entirely on assumption and guesswork. He even had to change established dates to make his theory work. Yet, he believed he was right. He began reconstructing the events at Roswell into what would become the mother of all flying saucer stories.

# ✦ 14 ✦

## Is This What Really Happened at Roswell?

In 1980, *The Roswell Incident* hit bookstores. Written by William Moore and Charles Berlitz (Friedman was an investigator on the project, Moore and Berlitz coauthored the book), it revealed for the first time what had really happened at Roswell . . . or at least, what Friedman had reconstructed. Here's what the book claimed:

In the spring and summer of 1947, saucer-shaped, interplanetary spaceships hovered over New Mexico. They wanted to keep track of humankind's scientific progress, and so they were drawn to the atomic and rocket research sites there. On the evening of July 2, one of these spaceships swooped low over Roswell. Not long after, it was struck by lightning, causing parts of the saucer to fall on Mack Brazel's ranch. The stricken spaceship managed to stay in the air for another 100 miles before crashing in an area of New Mexico called the Plains of San Agustin.

The next morning, July 3, Barney Barnett and a group of archaeologists came upon both the crashed saucer, and bodies of alien beings. The extraterrestrials were humanoids, about four feet tall. The military soon arrived. They kicked out the civilians with a warning to stay quiet about what they'd seen. Then they collected the wreckage and the bodies, and cleaned up all traces of the event.

That same day, Mack Brazel found the debris on his ranch. Two days passed before he learned from friends about the sightings of flying saucers in the area. Thinking the debris might be from one of them, he drove into Roswell the following morning, and reported his find to Sheriff George Wilcox. Wilcox, in turn, notified Roswell Army Air Field.

Major Jesse Marcel and another officer responded by going out to the Brazel's ranch. They collected the debris. It consisted of parchment-like material, and wooden beams—some of them printed with purplish symbols. These symbols were an extra-terrestrial form of writing, like hieroglyphics. Marcel also found paper-thin, lightweight sheets of silver metal. It couldn't be bent or burned. None of the material appeared to have come from Earth.

Marcel returned to the base. Either because of lax security, or part of a ruse to divert attention away from the crash site at San Agustin, public relations officer Walter Haut issued a press release announcing the discovery of the remains of a flying saucer. This news garnered national attention, but within hours General Roger Ramey denied it. He told the press that the wreckage was merely from a downed weather balloon. He also substituted the extraterrestrial wreckage for authentic bits of weather balloon to fool the press.

Both the press and the public accepted this cover story, concocted to hide the recovery of a spaceship and extraterrestrial bodies. The government concealed the truth in part to keep the public from panicking. It also considered the find a national security issue. That is, the military wanted to keep secret the advanced scientific knowledge it was gleaning from the spaceship, knowledge that might result in the ultimate secret weapon.

*The Roswell Incident* raised important questions about what to believe. How could readers evaluate the authors' claims? How could they decide whether they were credible?

The proven and most effective way was to use these basic principles of critical thinking:

1. "Extraordinary claims require extraordinary evidence": Simply put, this adage popularized by astronomer Carl Sagan (and known as the Sagan Standard) means that the evidence must be equal to the claim. Was the evidence presented in the book enough to support the

author's revolutionary claims? Did they have any other evidence besides those so-called "eyewitnesses?" Had they gone to great lengths to verify the truth of those accounts? And was there any physical evidence—photos, documents, or videos? When a scientist claims to have discovered a new kind of dinosaur, that scientist is asked to "show the body," or at least the bones and other pieces of convincing material. Could Friedman and Moore "show the body of the extraterrestrial," or "show the spaceship," or at least pieces of them?

2. Burden of proof: In a court of law, the prosecution must prove its case beyond a reasonable doubt, while the defense doesn't need to do anything to prove innocence. In science, extraordinary claims like Friedman and Moore's have a higher burden of proof than do routine

scientific advances, because it will overthrow a larger body of knowledge. Had the ufologists presented a high degree of proof—enough for humankind to reconsider much of what it knew about astronomy, biology, geology, and other sciences?

3. Occam's razor: This principle basically says that when there are two or more explanations for something that equally explain the facts, the simplest explanation is likely to be the best. One doesn't have to create overly complex explanations when simple ones might do. Occam's razor is especially helpful when evaluating two versions of an event. For example, which seems more likely: alien beings in sophisticated technology traveled many thousands of light years only to crash in the desert, or

that a government weather balloon fell apart above the Brazel ranch?

4. Authority: Were Moore, Berlitz, and Friedman experts on the subject? Friedman had worked as a nuclear physicist at General Electric Westinghouse, but he didn't hold a PhD in the subject. Did that matter? Did it matter that he didn't have training in any other relevant fields like meteorology or biology either? William Moore had been a high school language teacher before jumping into UFO research ten years earlier. Did that make him an expert? Charles Berlitz, a world-renowned linguist, wrote best sellers about paranormal phenomena like the Bermuda Triangle and the lost city of Atlantis. Could his claims be trusted?

5. Special pleading: When making their case, did the authors explain away lack of evidence with evasions like "the government's cover-up machine has clamped down on all documents," or "we may never be able to prove it because all traces have been hidden away"? Such special pleading is a sure sign the authors are trying to put forward a favored idea rather than verifiable fact.

Many readers ultimately decided *The Roswell Incident* was nonsense. No extraordinary evidence existed to support the author's claims. In truth, there was very little corroboration at all. Skeptics pointed out that the only reliable evidence was the original reports and photos from 1947—evidence the authors mostly rejected. In the book, Moore and Berlitz blamed the lack of proof on government lies and cover-ups. Additionally, most of the witnesses featured in the book had no credible connection to Roswell. Of the twenty-five people interviewed, only seven of them claimed to have seen the debris, and only five said they touched it: Floyd and Loretta Proctor, Bessie Brazel, her older brother Bill, and Jesse Marcel. All of them were trying to remember events more than thirty years in the past, making their testimony imperfect. Human memory is fallible. Research has shown that humans perceive things selectively, miss details, and even add to their memories. Some readers noted the similarity between the witnesses' descriptions of saucers and alien beings and those found in Frank Scully's debunked but famous book. Could they have mixed up those details with their own memories? It seemed possible.

The book, however, persuaded thousands of others. They now believed a spaceship *had* crashed near Roswell, and the government *had* covered it up. The public clamored to know more.

The lid was off Roswell, and the floodgates opened. Friedman, who continued to investigate the incident, became a lightning rod for people with their own Roswell stories. So did other self-declared ufologists longing to know the truth of the event. They placed ads in newspapers begging to speak with *anyone* who knew *anything*. Every lead was followed; every possible source was ferreted out. And with each discovery, ufologists reshaped the event. Most of these researchers stuck to the "core story." That is, they adhered to the version found in *The Roswell Incident* that Friedman had constructed from the testimony given by Jesse Marcel, Dan and Mary Grace Wilmot, and the Maltaises. They sought out witnesses with information they could add to this core story. Once they found it, they retold that core story, adding their "own revelations."

There was a problem, though. Most of witnesses' accounts were hearsay—second-, or even thirdhand accounts.

What was true? What wasn't? More than anything, ufologists needed irrefutable proof of an extraterrestrial crash. They needed incriminating evidence of a government cover-up.

If only they could find it.

## ✧ 15 ✧

## Real, or Fake?

On the night of December 11, 1984, documentary producer Jaime Shandera was reading in his Los Angeles home when he heard something drop through his mail slot. He went to investigate. There on the front hall floor lay a brown envelope. He picked it up. Who was it from? Strangely, the envelope did not include a return address. Shandera opened it. Inside was a roll of undeveloped photo film, nothing else.

Baffled, the producer put the mysterious film into his jacket pocket. Coincidentally, he happened to be meeting his friend William Moore, the UFO investigator and coauthor of *The Roswell Incident*, for dinner. But when he arrived at the restaurant and told Moore about the film, the ufologist insisted they ditch the meal. Instead, they drove to Moore's house, where they developed the film.

The photographs turned out to be eight pages of top secret documents. And the tale they told—if authentic—was explosive. One memo described a number of extraterrestrial encounters, including the Roswell crash, from 1947 on into the 1950s. These claims, however, were so vague they could be easily dismissed. The real gold in the documents was the revelation that President Harry Truman had established a supersecret group of twelve men made up of scientists, politicians, and government officials. Code-named "Majestic-12," the group's job was to figure out how to deal with the Roswell crash, as well as any future encounters with alien beings. Another memo confirmed the reconstructed story set down by Moore and Berlitz in *The Roswell Incident*. It read:

> "On 07 July, 1947 a secret operation was begun [to retrieve wreckage from Brazel's

*ranch]. During the course of this operation, aerial reconnaissance discovered that four small humanlike beings . . . had fallen to earth about two miles east of the [debris] site . . . A special scientific team took charge of removing these bodies for study . . . The wreckage of the craft was removed to several different locations . . . news reporters were given the effective story that the object had been a misguided research balloon . . ."*

Moore was exuberant. Here, at last, was irrefutable proof. A secret government cabal *had* covered up America's first encounter with extraterrestrials. And it confirmed the scenario he put forth in *The Roswell Incident*!

Word of the document's existence soon got around the UFO community. Not waiting for verification of the documents' authenticity, many chose to believe their contents. M-12 became part of the Roswell story.

Others, however, examined the documents and

noticed inconsistencies. Some of the Majestic-12 members had incorrect military rank assignments, and the memo's formatting looked wrong. It just didn't match other standard government documents from the same time period. But perhaps the most suspicious thing about the documents was their origin. Where had they come from? It seemed too convenient for such important papers to suddenly "drop on a doorstep like something out of a fairy tale," wrote Carl Sagan. Some people thought William Moore had had the documents forged.

The Air Force got wind of them. They launched an investigation into their authenticity. Had they really come from government archives? If so, were they still classified? The FBI looked into the matter, too. It took agents less than a month to determine the documents were "fabricated and completely bogus." Among other technical reasons, they noted that the signatures in M-12 had been copied from other documents. To hammer home the point that they were fakes, FBI agents scrawled the world "bogus" across all eight pages in big capital letters.

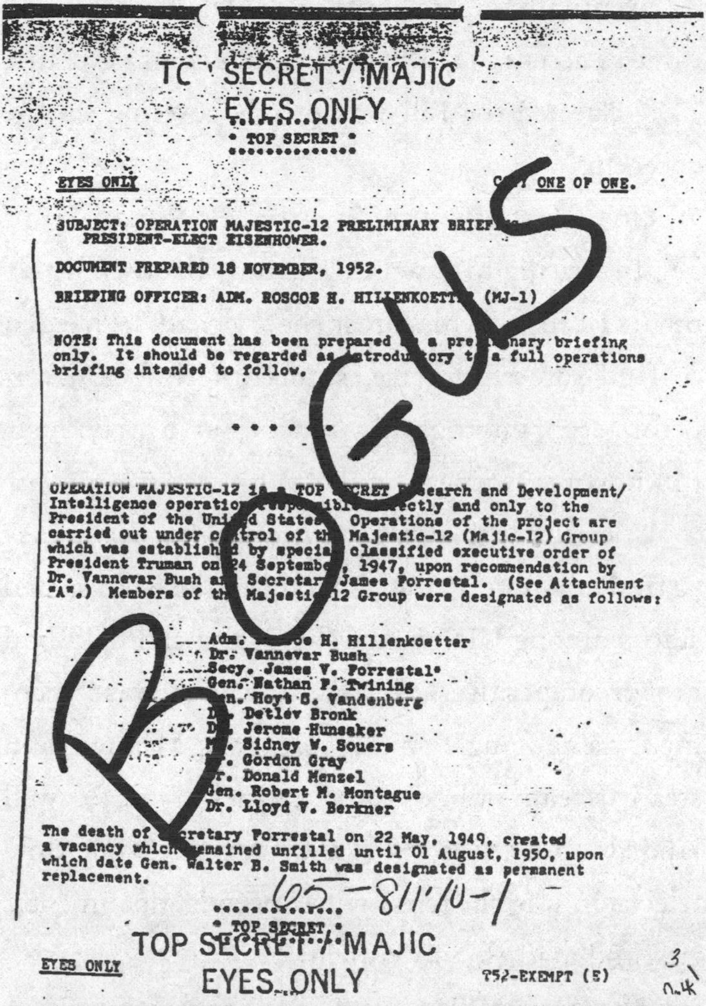

TOP SECRET / MAJIC
EYES ONLY

• TOP SECRET •

EYES ONLY

COPY ONE OF ONE.

SUBJECT: OPERATION MAJESTIC-12 PRELIMINARY BRIEFING FOR PRESIDENT-ELECT EISENHOWER.

DOCUMENT PREPARED 18 NOVEMBER, 1952.

BRIEFING OFFICER: ADM. ROSCOE H. HILLENKOETTER (MJ-1)

NOTE: This document has been prepared as a preliminary briefing only. It should be regarded as introductory to a full operations briefing intended to follow.

• • • • • •

OPERATION MAJESTIC-12 is a TOP SECRET Research and Development/ Intelligence operation responsible directly and only to the President of the United States. Operations of the project are carried out under control of the Majestic-12 (Majic-12) Group which was established by special classified executive order of President Truman on 24 September, 1947, upon recommendation by Dr. Vannevar Bush and Secretary James Forrestal. (See Attachment "A".) Members of the Majestic-12 Group were designated as follows:

Adm. Roscoe H. Hillenkoetter
Dr. Vannevar Bush
Secy. James V. Forrestal*
Gen. Nathan F. Twining
Gen. Hoyt S. Vandenberg
Dr. Detlev Bronk
Dr. Jerome Hunsaker
Mr. Sidney W. Souers
Mr. Gordon Gray
Dr. Donald Menzel
Gen. Robert M. Montague
Dr. Lloyd V. Berkner

The death of Secretary Forrestal on 22 May, 1949, created a vacancy which remained unfilled until 01 August, 1950, upon which date Gen. Walter B. Smith was designated as permanent replacement.

BOGUS

65-81110-1

• • • • • •
• TOP SECRET •

TOP SECRET / MAJIC
EYES ONLY

EYES ONLY

T52-EXEMPT (E)

A page from the FBI's Majestic-12 file with the bureau's conclusion writ large across it.

Eventually, most people in the UFO community came to accept the FBI's verdict. But some never did. They claimed the FBI was merely covering up the cover-up.

One of those was Stanton Friedman. He'd begun writing his own book, and the M-12 documents fit in with his latest theory. Still, he needed to find something else, something big—a never-before-seen photograph, maybe, or a previously unknown eyewitness.

Unfortunately, new revelations were not as easy to find anymore. Roswell had been raised to sacred status among UFO researchers, and the field had grown competitive. Everyone, it seemed, was searching for a new angle on the core story. Meanwhile, a steady stream of books and articles about Roswell landed on shelves and newsstands. Prime-time television was cluttered with specials, documentaries, and made-for-TV movies.

On January 24, 1990, a national television program called *Unsolved Mysteries* rebroadcast an episode about Roswell. In it, Friedman, who appeared during a segment of the show, described the crashed saucer with its dead crew lying on the sand. At program's end, producers displayed a toll-free telephone number on the screen. Those with tips were encouraged to call. Minutes after the broadcast, the TV network's phone line rang.

The caller remembered both the saucer crash and the bodies of alien beings. He remembered what his astonished brother had said at the time, too: "'That's a [gosh-durned] spaceship! Them's Martians!'"

## ✧ 16 ✧

## Can a Five-Year-Old Remember All This?

July 5, 1947, was oven hot, recalled Gerald Anderson. He'd ridden in the back seat of his Uncle Ted's Buick for what seemed like hours. Eventually, they stopped and hiked across the plains of San Agustin—himself, his father and brother, Uncle Ted, and his cousin Victor—in search of moss agates. Just five years old at the time, Gerald was tired. He trudged along, wishing he had a bottle of cold soda. Instead, he got something far more astonishing.

Stanton Friedman stopped him for a moment. Was the camera rolling? It was. Friedman looked directly into it. He introduced himself. "I'm here in Kansas City, Missouri," he said, "to do an interview with . . . a very important witness with regard to the recovery of a crashing flying saucer in New Mexico in July 1947 . . ." The ufologist could barely contain his excitement. Thank goodness he'd caught the tip from *Unsolved Mysteries. This* was the proof he'd been searching for. *This* was the testimony that would break the Roswell case wide open. He cleared his throat and noted on tape and for the record that Anderson had taken a lie detector test and passed. "So with that," he said, "we will talk with Gerald Anderson."

The rock hunters saw it after hiking over an arroyo, Anderson continued, a crashed flying saucer, its silver metal glinting in the sunlight, the wide gash in its side exposing an interior of blinking colors. In the shade of the wreckage lay three dead creatures. Beside them, surrounded by several strange-shaped boxes, sat a live one. To Gerald, it appeared to have been giving first aid to the others. But when it saw the hikers approach, the creature froze. Then it drew back in fear and covered its head with its hands.

"What did [the creatures] look like?" asked Friedman.

Anderson answered smoothly. They were short, just 4 or 4 ½ feet tall with large tapering heads, and almond-shaped black eyes that were so dark and shiny they had "a bluish tint when light reflected off them." The creatures had no visible ears, their noses were nothing but two holes, and their mouths looked "like a cut," just a straight line.

The living creature didn't make any sounds, not even as they moved closer. Anderson remembered his Uncle Ted trying to talk with the creature, first in Spanish, then in sign language. It didn't understand a word, but it calmed. It laid its four-fingered hands in its lap and looked from person to person.

Finally, its dark gaze fell on Anderson. Instantly, the boy's mind exploded with feelings of sadness and despair—emotions he'd never experienced before. Was the creature communicating with him?

Could it be that Anderson picked up the creature's feelings because he was a child? Was this terrible sadness how the alien being felt? Anderson speculated aloud about all this.

Friedman, however, didn't offer his opinion, and after a few minutes, Anderson continued.

His cousin Victor tried to squeeze in through the saucer's gash. He wanted to see inside. But the adults pulled him back. What if the machine exploded? It was better the boy stayed clear. Victor argued with them. He was still grumbling when a group of college-aged people—"three boys and two girls"—appeared. Led by an older man they called Dr. Buskirk, they explained they were archaeology students. Almost at the same time, a pickup truck arrived, and a man wearing brown clothes, boots, and a straw hat climbed out. Anderson hadn't known it at the time, but after watching the *Unsolved Mysteries* episode, he now believed the man was Barney Barnett.

Friedman thought so, too.

What happened next?

A rendition of what Gerald Anderson claimed to have seen as a five-year-old boy.

They all looked at the crash. Some of the students even pocketed pieces of the saucer. Anderson recalled one of the girls picking up a glowing red stone. "Wouldn't this make a pretty ring?" he remembered her saying.

Then suddenly, the site swarmed with military— trucks, jeeps, even planes. "Get away! Get away!" soldiers shouted. They pointed their guns at the group of civilians.

One particularly nasty captain with red hair threatened them. "This is a military secret," Anderson recalled him hollering. Anyone who breathed a word of what they'd just seen would be locked in prison for life. Did they understand? Then Anderson and the others were marched off the site.

The camera stopped filming. What a thrilling firsthand account. It more than corroborated what the Maltaises had told Friedman years earlier. It would be even better, however, if Anderson had some documentary evidence to back it up. A photograph perhaps?

Anderson shook his head. None of them had brought along a camera that day. But he did have something else—his Uncle Ted's diary. His uncle had written about the event at the time.

A few days later, Anderson handed over the diary. Friedman could not contain his delight. Uncle Ted's diary entry perfectly corroborated his nephew's story.

Other ufologists, however, didn't buy his story. Anderson's total recall of conversations, his vivid details, his spot-on estimates of the distances between objects on the ground strained their belief. Anderson had been a kindergartner at the time he said the event happened. Was a memory like that even possible?

Two competing UFO researchers, Kevin Randle and Donald Schmitt, went so far as to hire a forensic scientist to examine the 1947 diary. The results? The diary was, indeed, written on bona fide 1947-vintage paper. However, the *ink* on that paper had not become available until 1974.

"Clearly this was not a document written by Anderson's Uncle Ted," Randle and Schmitt wrote triumphantly in their own book, *The Truth About the UFO Crash at Roswell,* published in 1991. Ted Anderson could not be reached for comment. He had died several years prior to 1974.

Randle and Schmitt believed they'd exposed Gerald Anderson's story as a hoax. But Stanton Friedman stood by his witness. At the same time, he continued looking for someone who could back up Anderson's outstanding memory. He never found anyone.

That didn't stop him, however, from including Anderson's claims in his 1994 book *Crash at Corona* (coauthored with UFO buff Don Berliner). Based on Anderson's "exclusive testimony," as well as the debunked M-12 documents, which Friedman hyped as "new evidence of the government's secret . . . team," and statements from even more new witnesses, he reconstructed the Roswell events again. This time he alleged that *two* flying saucers had crashed, and eight alien beings had been found—two of who survived and were hidden by the US government.

Could anyone top that story?

## ✦ 17 ✦

## A Top Secret Group of Nine?

His real name was Frank Kaufmann, although he went by several aliases—Steve McKenzie, Joseph Osborne, and Mr. X. He first surfaced in 1991, and for nearly a decade he mesmerized ufologists with his revelations.

"It was the blips, see?" he told Kevin Randle. Blips on a radar screen. That's what got him involved with the Roswell incident. In July 1947, Kaufmann was stationed at Roswell Army Air Field when he received orders from a high-ranking general: Head over to White Sands and establish a radar watch.

What was the general's name?

Kaufmann refused to tell.

Airmen monitored the sky in the 1940s using radar equipment that looked like this.

Why had he caught the assignment?

Kaufmann acted uncomfortable. He looked around at the landscape paintings on the wall. He'd done them himself.

Randle and Schmitt waited patiently for an answer. They'd been visiting Kaufmann in his

Roswell home for months now as he parceled out his story in bits. Was it secrecy or shyness? He'd hinted that there were consequences if he told all he knew. And the ufologists sensed there was much to be revealed.

Finally, he answered. He'd been part of a nine-member special team called "The Group of Nine." The Nine possessed the highest of government clearances possible. Even the president of the United States didn't know the things they did. Exceptionally trained in various fields, these men had been brought together to investigate UFO crashes, as well as clean up any messes made by them. By July 1947, the big brass knew something strange was happening in the skies over New Mexico. They wanted Kaufmann on it. And he went.

The minute he saw those radar blips he knew no ordinary aircraft had caused them. Right away, he notified The Nine and told them to get ready. At one point during his watch, a violent thunderstorm blew in. Suddenly, "the radar screen lit up with a tremendous flash." Then the blip disappeared.

Kaufmann knew what that meant. The craft had been struck by lightning and crashed.

The Nine roared into action. Kaufmann hurried back to the Roswell base where the other members were already waiting, having flown in by military jet from Washington, DC.

Now they raced to the crash site. They knew where the craft had landed based on those radar blips. Taking two army vehicles, they drove thirty-five miles north of Roswell. "On an old ranch road I spied a glow over the horizon," said Kaufmann. They'd arrived at the site.

The spectacle stunned The Nine. In a ravine lay the "split open spaceship." V-shaped, it had a dome in the middle. Outside the ship lay two bodies—one sprawled on the ground, the other next to a cliff. "That's the one I cannot forget," said Kaufmann. "It had [a] serene look on its face . . . like it was at peace with the world . . . I [was] amazed at that."

As military police cordoned off the area and took up security positions, The Nine hung back. "We were all talking about how we were going to handle this thing," claimed Kaufmann. Finally, they descended into the ravine and went inside the downed spaceship. They found three more bodies.

What did they look like, asked the ufologists.

Kaufman claimed they looked a lot like humans, but they weren't. They were proportionally smaller and thinner, and their eyes were slightly larger than human eyes. But their hands were "normal," with four fingers and a thumb. The middle finger was *not* elongated. The main difference, noted Kaufmann,

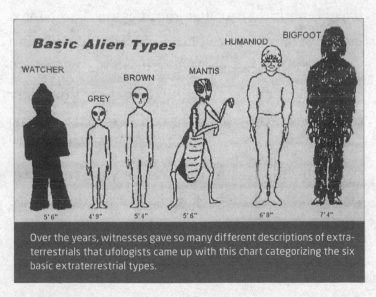

### Basic Alien Types

WATCHER

GREY

BROWN

MANTIS

HUMANIOD

BIGFOOT

5' 6"    4' 9"    5' 4"    5' 6"    6' 8"    7' 4"

Over the years, witnesses gave so many different descriptions of extra-terrestrials that ufologists came up with this chart categorizing the six basic extraterrestrial types.

was the skin color. Extraterrestrials had "paler, grayish skin."

Then what happened?

"The medical MPs" recovered the bodies and sealed them in lead-lined bags. After being placed in the rear of a military ambulance, they were whisked to Roswell Army Air Field. At the base hospital, military pathologists examined the bodies. Then orderlies placed all five in a large, wooden crate and carried it out to an empty airplane hangar. Kaufmann noted with pride that the hangar had been cleared in just minutes on The Nine's orders. Military police placed the crate in the middle of the hangar, trained a spotlight on it and stationed themselves around the hangar's interior, their rifles at the ready. The bodies stayed this way overnight.

Meanwhile, back at the crash site, a twenty-man detail recovered the spaceship and all the debris. This went by flatbed truck to the base, where it was loaded onto transport planes. They were flown to

Wright Field (soon to become Wright-Patterson Air Force Base) in Dayton, Ohio.

Randle wondered about the size of the spaceship.

It was big, Kaufmann replied, twenty-five feet long and fifteen feet across at its widest place.

That *was* big. Had the military taken it apart before transport?

No, said Kaufmann, it was not dismantled.

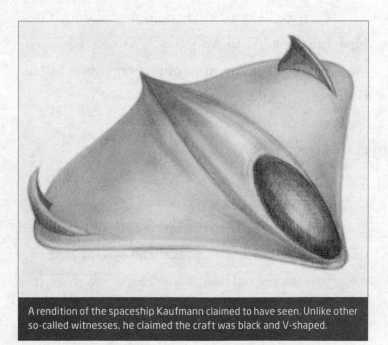

A rendition of the spaceship Kaufmann claimed to have seen. Unlike other so-called witnesses, he claimed the craft was black and V-shaped.

What about the extraterrestrial bodies? Where did they go?

Here Kaufmann's memory seemed to turn foggy. At some point the bodies were flown out of Roswell. They had different destinations. He did remember The Nine ordering two planes to carry them. That way if there was an accident, not all the bodies would be lost.

Of course, he went along on one of these airlifts. His plane headed to Andrews Air Force Base near Washington, DC. "Some people there wanted to see the body," he said slyly.

President Harry Truman?

"Maybe," replied Kaufmann.

Army Chief of Staff Dwight Eisenhower?

"He might have taken a peek."

His flight, Kaufmann claimed, then continued on to Wright Field. Eventually, the other plane carrying extraterrestrial bodies touched down there, too.

Back in Roswell, the remaining members of The Nine made sure they covered their tracks. All those

What lurks inside seemingly ordinary Building 18 on Wright-Patterson Air Force Base? Some witnesses, like Frank Kaufmann, claimed the Roswell flying saucer, as well as the alien beings' bodies, were stashed in Hangar 18. But officials at Wright-Patterson insist he and the others must have made a mistake. According to officials at Wright-Patterson, there is no Hangar 18, just this place ... Building 18. And inside the building? Offices, not extraterrestrials.

involved in the cleanup were debriefed and warned to keep their mouths shut unless "they wanted to spend time in the brig." Camouflage experts arrived to put the desert earth back to the way it had been before the crash. They even swept away the tracks made by the military vehicles.

What about Mack Brazel and his debris field? Did Kaufmann know anything about that?

Kaufmann shrugged. It was just a diversion. The Air Force *wanted* the press to focus attention on the Brazel story, and away from the *real* news—that a spaceship had crashed thirty-five miles north of Roswell and bodies had been recovered. The press release was a diversion, too. The Nine purposely created it to cause a stir. They devised General Ramey's balloon explanation as well, which caused another stir.

Kaufmann grinned. They'd been so clever.

"Know what else was fake?" he said. The debris field found on the ranch. The Nine created the fake site to mislead anyone who got too near to the real site . . . or the real story.

It was a fascinating tale. But could it possibly be true?

Randle and Schmitt dug into it, looking for corroboration. What they found disturbed them. Official military records showed that Kaufmann had been out of uniform since 1945. Yes, he'd still worked at Roswell Army Air Field in 1947, but as a personnel clerk, doing typing and filing. Surely, this proved he was lying.

Not so fast, replied Kaufmann when they confronted him with their find. He'd done nominal duties to keep up appearances. The job was part of his cover. In fact, he worked for counterintelligence. In other words, he was a spy.

The ufologists pressured him to provide some proof.

Kaufmann did. He handed over his TOP SECRET OFFICIAL REPORT on Roswell.

Randle and Schmitt examined it. The letterhead on the report's first page *did* look like that used in 1947. If only they could forensically test it for authenticity. Unfortunately, Kaufmann had given them a photocopy. They needed the original to verify the age of the paper and ink. Time and again, they asked Kaufmann for it.

He never handed it over.

But he did produce other documents confirming his story. He showed Randle and Schmitt his logbook from July 1947. An entry dated July 4 read:

"Object Down—2317 [meaning 11:17 p.m.] RADAR THREAT GONE."

He also produced a letter written by Major Edwin Easley dated July 30, 1947, that included the subject line "Recovery, Flying Discs." It read, in part:

"The craft recovered is assumed to be a manned craft of unknown origin and may in fact represent an interplanetary craft . . ."

These documents looked genuine. But like that top secret report, they could not be tested. They, too, were photocopies.

Randle would later admit their investigation revealed a few flaws. "But every time we began to doubt, or ask difficult questions, Kaufmann would provide a little bit of documentation along with broad hints that he had much more. He said, repeatedly, that when the time came, he had the documents to prove what he said."

Kaufmann's testimony was challenged almost from the moment it was reported. Competition among those investigating Roswell had become contentious. Ufologists often attacked each other's witnesses, calling them names like "clown" and "liar." At conferences, and in books and articles, they squabbled over crash sites, the descriptions of saucers, and the number and condition of the extra-terrestrial bodies. They found Kaufmann's story especially controversial. "If what he said was true, then certain other events could not be," explained Randle. It would prove Stanton Friedman wrong about there being two crash sites. It would debunk the story of Barney Barnett and the archaeologists stumbling across extraterrestrial wreckage. In fact, it would change the whole core story!

Ufologists magnified little things in Kaufmann's story with the suggestion that he couldn't be trusted. He'd said, for example, that radar at the Roswell base had also tracked the object. But no one could confirm if Roswell had radar capability in 1947. Kauffman had also said he'd watched on the radar screen as the target was stuck by lightning. But in those days, a target struck by lightning would only show up on the screen if it hit at exactly the same time the radar beam swept across the target. Impossible? No. Improbable? Highly. And then there was Kaufmann's assertion that the wrecked airship had been flown to Wright Field without being taken apart. That couldn't have happened, researchers pointed out. Summed up one ufologist, "In 1947, and for years after, there was no aircraft in the world, let alone in the American military, capable of accommodating an object of those dimensions."

To Randle and Schmitt's minds, these were quibbles. They accepted Kaufmann's story. Eventually, his testimony would add a weight of new evidence to the two books the men coauthored: *UFO Crash at Roswell* (1991) and *The Truth About the UFO Crash at Roswell* (1994).

But the debate in the UFO community continued. Was there a witness *everyone* believed?

There *was* one man. And they were convinced his story was the key to the whole Roswell riddle.

## ✦ 18 ✦

## The Truth, or a Tall Tale?

In July 1947, Glenn Dennis was fresh out of mortuary school. The twenty-two-year-old undertaker and hearse driver worked at Ballard Funeral Home in Roswell. Since the funeral home had a contract with the army to provide funeral services, it wasn't unusual to receive phone calls from the air base. But on the afternoon of July 7, at around 1:30, a mortuary officer telephoned with a series of baffling questions. How did one preserve a body that had been exposed to the elements? Did the funeral home have any child-sized coffins? Were those coffins airtight? And most importantly, what were the effects of embalming fluid on dead tissue?

Glenn Dennis in 1947.

Dennis asked if there was a problem. Had something happened? Should he come to the base?

No, no, said the caller. He was merely asking, "in case something comes up in the future." He clicked off.

Odd, thought Dennis.

The funeral home's phone rang again. This time it was an emergency call. There'd been a motorcycle accident involving an airman from the base. Since the funeral home also operated the town's ambulance (a common practice in those days) Dennis raced to the site.

After collecting the wounded airman, Dennis drove him to the base hospital. Three army ambulances were already parked at the entrance, their back doors open. As Dennis wheeled his patient up the ramp, he looked inside the vehicles. Wreckage! "It resembled stainless steel with a purple hue," he recalled, "as if it had been exposed to high temperatures." There was some strange-looking writing on the material, too, that reminded him of Egyptian hieroglyphs.

Dennis signed in the airman, then strolled toward the lounge to get a Coke. The typically quiet hallways buzzed with activity. Officers dashed between rooms; nurses raced around. He wondered if there'd been a plane crash. That would explain the earlier telephone calls. Maybe he should ask if they needed his undertaking services. He turned a corner.

"Don't move from here," barked an officer. He pointed at Dennis. "Don't take one step." He walked away, but moments later returned with two military police. "Get this man off base," he told the MPs. "He's off limits."

The military police flanked Dennis. Grabbing his arms, they walked him back down the hall. But they'd only gone a few feet when a voice shouted, "Bring him back here."

Dennis and the MPs stopped and turned. Before them loomed a redheaded captain, a cruel expression in his eyes. Beside him stood an equally menacing sergeant.

The captain stepped forward and poked Dennis in the chest with his finger. "Look mister," he growled. "You don't go into Roswell and start a bunch of rumors that there's been a crash. Nothing has happened here, you understand?"

"I'm a civilian and you can't do anything to me," retorted Dennis.

The captain poked him again. "Somebody will be picking your bones out of the sand."

"Sir, he would make better dog food," piped up the sergeant.

"Get him out of here," ordered the captain.

The MPs turned Dennis around and started leading him away.

The door to the supply room opened and out

stumbled a nurse. It was Naomi Self, a friend of Dennis's. She pressed a towel over her mouth and nose, and her eyes were wide with fear. When she saw Dennis, she screamed, "Glenn! Get out of here as fast as you can!" Then sobbing, gasping for air, she made her way across the hall and into another room.

The military police tightened their grip on Dennis's arms. They wrangled him out the door and into his ambulance. Following him back to the funeral home, they warned him to stay away from the base.

Their treatment left Dennis sputtering with anger. But he felt worried, too. Once inside the funeral home, he hurried to the telephone and dialed the base hospital. He wanted to make sure Naomi was all right. But the officer who answered claimed she wasn't there. So Dennis telephoned the nurse's quarters. She wasn't there either. He left her a message.

Not until the next morning did she call back.

She sounded sick and frantic. She *had* to talk with him. Please! Could he meet her at the officer's club on base?

Dennis drove straight there. Naomi was standing outside waiting for him, and they walked in together. Even though the place wasn't busy, they took a corner table. She looked nervous and disheveled, and her eyes were puffy from crying. She wanted to know what the MPs had done to him.

He told her about their harassment. "But I don't know why," he added.

"Well, I'll tell you why," she said. She told him about being in the operating room when two doctors she'd never seen before unzipped the body bag that was laying on the stainless steel table. A horrible stench rose from the bag. It was so awful it made her want to vomit. Still, she looked inside. Two small, mangled bodies lay there. The doctors used forceps to turn over one of the creature's hands. It had only four fingers, and there were little, suction cup–like pads on the tips. Their mouths were slits, about an inch long, and toothless. Two small holes made up their noses, while their large, sunken eyes covered most of their face. Their heads were large, their bodies small.

Dennis shook his head. It was hard to imagine.

So Naomi drew him pictures of what she'd seen on the back of a prescription pad. She gave them to Dennis. "Guard them with your life," she told him. The undertaker thought maybe his having them

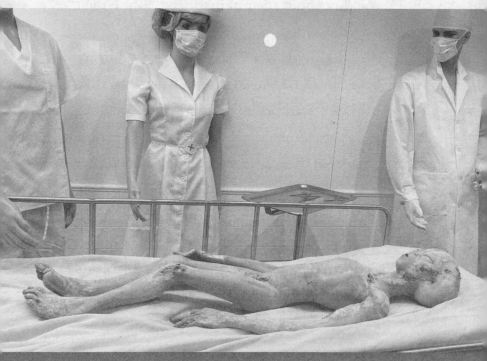

This recreation of the autopsy as described by Glenn Dennis can be found at the International UFO Museum in Roswell.

was for her protection. Why else would she give them to him?

She continued. She'd heard rumors about where the bodies went after the examination, she said. First, they'd been moved to a hangar and then flown to Wright Field.

Dennis wondered where the creatures had been found.

Naomi had an answer. She'd overhead the doctors saying they'd been pulled from some wreckage that had been found some miles out of town.

Naomi abruptly stood. She had to go on shift. Dennis stood, too. He put the drawings in his pocket. Would she be all right? He hoped so.

Later that day, Dennis went into his office to write an obituary. The day's paper was lying on the desk. He read the headline: "RAAF Captures Flying Saucer on Ranch in Roswell Region."

"Maybe," he thought, "that's what Naomi had gotten into!"

He tried contacting her the next day, but she couldn't come to the phone. He called the day after, and she still couldn't talk. He struck out the third day, too. So he drove to the base hospital.

Naomi wasn't there. According to her commanding officer, she'd been shipped out the same day he'd spoken with her at the officer's club. For the next six weeks, he didn't hear a word from her. Then a letter arrived. She was in England, she wrote, but didn't have time to compose a long letter. She just wanted to give him her new mailing address, and make sure nothing had happened to him. The letter didn't have a signature at the bottom, just a typed name. "To tell you the truth," said Dennis, "I don't think it came from her. I think somebody wrote it to try and find out what I knew."

Dennis sent a letter to her new address. He told her he was okay, and she should write when she had time.

Another six weeks went by before the letter he'd written to Naomi landed back in his mailbox. Stamped in black on the front of the envelope were the words "Return to Sender." And in the corner, stamped in red, was a single word: "Deceased."

At the base, they told him what had happened.

What happened to the alien bodies? Some ufologists have claimed—without a shred of evidence—that the government had them preserved in special incubator-type containers like this one re-created at the International UFO Museum in Roswell.

Naomi had gone down in a plane on a training mission. She'd been killed with some other nurses. Dennis, however, wasn't sure he believed it.

Back in his office, and feeling suddenly nervous, he took out a file folder and wrote the word PERSONAL across its front. He put both letters, as well as Naomi's drawings, inside. Then he hid the folder among his personal files in the funeral home's basement. No one would ever find them there.

# Can a Ufologist Fool Himself?

Nine-year old Karl Pflock saw a UFO in the summer of 1952. He'd been out fishing with his father and three friends when an object appeared in the California sky. The triangle-shaped craft didn't make a sound as it hovered above them. Pflock shaded his eyes with his hand and watched as it rotated a full 360 degrees before whooshing away. What was it? After considering the possibilities—bright star, airplane, rocket, flares, even a balloon—they concluded it was a UFO.

Just months earlier, the boy had read an article in the April 1952 issue of *Life* magazine called "Have We Visitors from Space?"

He'd shouted his answer when he got to the end. "Yes!"

Karl Pflock believed.

Forty years later, he still did. But his years working in the Department of Defense and as an intelligence officer with the CIA had left him both open-minded and hardheaded about UFOs. He'd studied reams of sighting reports and evaluated thousands of witness testimonies. And while he found most of them interesting—and even wished some were true—he couldn't take the majority of them seriously. "My brain wouldn't let me get away with self-delusion, at least not for long," he once explained.

As a UFO researcher, he paid little attention to anything he'd didn't regard as "Serious Stuff." And he cared not a whit for fellow ufologists. He found them—with rare exceptions like Stanton Friedman and Kevin Randle—lacking in "objectivity, competence, integrity, and sometimes even sanity." He believed they used wishful thinking instead of critical thinking in their attempts to solve the UFO

Karl Pflock in 1987, taken by the Department of Defense.

mysteries. Because of that, they were often taken in by the "alleged recollections of witnesses." This had muddled the whole ufology field. It had become, claimed Pflock, a "big circus labeled 'UFO.'" How would they ever learn the truth this way?

And more than anything, Pflock wanted to know the truth.

169

To his mind, nothing was more tangled and messy than the Roswell investigation. All those contradictions! All those extraordinary claims! It was time for a fresh evaluation of the incident, he decided. Using critical thinking and solid investigative practices, he would reexamine all the evidence. He would review all the witness accounts.

Pflock's lived by the motto: "Consider everything, believe nothing." So he was open to the possibility that saucers really had crashed outside Roswell. But he went into his investigation utterly objective. Or at least he thought so.

He kicked off his project with Glenn Dennis's testimony. Of the many eyewitness accounts Pflock had read, the one he was the most skeptical of was the undertaker's. Stanton Friedman—who'd been the first to talk with the undertaker back in 1989—had videotaped their interview. Pflock now asked to borrow the unedited version. Friedman generously obliged.

It arrived soon afterward. Pflock hurried into his home office in Placitas, New Mexico. He pushed the videotape into the player. Seconds later, Glenn

Dennis appeared on the TV screen. His hair was gray, and he wore blue jeans and a plaid shirt that strained a bit over his potbelly. In his folksy drawl, he told his bizarre tale.

Pflock found himself shaking his head. It sounded like the plot of a bad horror movie.

At one point, Dennis said, "If someone else was telling this story, I wouldn't believe him."

Pflock laughed out loud. "Would you buy a car from that guy?" he asked himself.

"No way!" he answered.

A few months afterward, in December 1992, he met and interviewed Dennis for the first time. Despite himself, Pflock was impressed. Maybe he'd jumped to conclusions. In fact, the more he got to know Dennis, the more he liked and trusted him. Folks in Roswell certainly respected him. And while some found Dennis's story hard to swallow, they brushed away their doubts by saying things like "If Glenn said it happened, then you can bet it did."

Pflock—with very little corroborating evidence— *did* bet it happened. "I was convinced Dennis was telling the truth as best as he could remember it," he said.

But his doubts about the undertaker reemerged when Dennis began giving interviews—to the Associated Press, as well as a TV investigator from Ohio, and *American Funeral Director*, a national magazine for morticians. In these retellings, Dennis included a detail he'd never mentioned before. He now said the doctors described by Naomi Self were pathologists from Walter Reed Hospital, the army's medical facility in Washington, DC.

Pflock found this puzzling. If army pathologists had been on the scene in 1947, why did anyone need to call and ask Dennis's advice about the effects of embalming fluid on tissue? Pathologists would certainly have known the answer.

He telephoned Dennis and asked him about it.

Dennis said he'd been misquoted.

Pflock hung up the phone, feeling a twinge of suspicion. He riffled through his investigation notes. Was there *any* physical evidence to back up Dennis's story?

Not for the first time, Pflock wished Dennis still had the nurse's drawings and letters—the ones he'd hidden among the basement files. But Dennis claimed to have left the file behind when he retired from the undertaking business. Years later when he went back to get it, he discovered that all the basement files had been shredded and burned.

Pflock had accepted this story. He'd considered it unfortunate. Now, he wondered if it was too convenient: a conclusive piece of evidence . . . gone!

Also conveniently missing was the person Dennis claimed was a firsthand witness to bodies of alien beings—Naomi Self. Other ufologists had looked for her, but with no luck. "Once again it appears as if [government agents] really covered their tracks," declared one. In a weird twist of what Pflock called "saucer logic," not being able to locate the nurse had actually bolstered Dennis's story. The lack of evidence *became* evidence.

Pflock didn't accept this "saucer logic." There had to be some clues to her whereabouts. He decided to enlist the help of an influential friend, a United States congressman, to get ahold of her service records.

But when he told Dennis about the plan, the undertaker balked. He'd had a "flash recollection," he told Pflock. He now remembered he'd spelled her name wrong. It wasn't Self, but Selff, double *f*. He also suddenly remembered her middle name, too: Maria.

Pflock felt hopeful. With her full name—Naomi Maria Selff—he might just be able to locate her.

It was an exhaustive search. Victor Golubic, a diligent ufologist and friend of Pflock's, searched for any record of her in the *Roswell Army Air Force Yearbook*. He found records for *every* nurse who'd served there in 1947. But not one of those nurses was named Naomi Maria Selff. Nor was there anyone with a name slightly resembling it.

Could Dennis provide any more clues?

The undertaker searched his memory. He remembered she came from Minnesota.

Golubic traveled to St. Paul. He did a genealogical search of Minnesota families with the last name of

Selff, or anything similar. Again, he came up with nothing.

Could they find her in the files of the World War II Cadet Nurse Corps? The corps held the membership cards for 125,000 female nurses who'd served in the military between 1942 and 1948. Golubic looked. Yet again, he found nothing.

After pulling some government strings, Pflock managed to get his hands on the Roswell Army Air Field's "morning reports," from 1946 to 1947. These lengthy reports listed all personnel going on or returning from leave, reporting for duty, or transferring out. Naomi Selff wasn't in any of them.

In the fall of 1995, a discouraged Pflock told Dennis he had a problem. Naomi Selff didn't appear to be a real person.

Dennis said he wasn't surprised. Naomi Selff had never been her real name. He hadn't told Pflock the truth, he claimed, because he didn't trust him.

By now, Pflock didn't trust Dennis either.

Another Roswell researcher came forward. Dennis had told him the nurse's name was Naomi Snipes. Could that be true?

Pflock didn't believe it. It was too close to Naomi Selff, and would have been spotted in Golubic's search.

During a later interview, Dennis—obviously feeling pressed—said he'd never told *anyone* her real name. In fact, her last name didn't even start with *S*.

And in one of their last conversations, he said, "I promised her I would never reveal her real name, so I can't confirm or deny. If she's alive, I don't want her to get in any more trouble . . . If I ever got proof she was dead, I probably would make her name known or confirm it."

Pflock abandoned Dennis as a credible witness. "Baloney by any other name—Nurse Naomi Selff, if you like—is still baloney," he said.

Still, the incident embarrassed Pflock. He believed he'd come into the investigation thinking critically, using solid investigative practices and being objective. Instead, he had turned a blind eye to

Dennis's ridiculous story. He'd ignored clues. He'd brushed aside doubts. It was all completely contrary to his CIA training. Why hadn't he applied his motto: Consider everything, but believe nothing?

"Because of an overwhelming will to believe," he concluded.

And that, he realized, was the problem with the research into Roswell. Ufologists wanted to believe so badly that it had happened, they'd forgotten to take the truth seriously, and follow the facts wherever they led . . . even if that meant admitting that flying saucers had never crashed outside that New Mexico town.

## Wait . . . Is *This* What Really Happened at Roswell?

Walter Haut, the public relations officer who'd issued the press release about the capture of a flying saucer, still lived in Roswell. By 1995, the retired army officer worked at a new job—president of the International UFO Museum and Research Center.

With the sudden and immense interest in the saucer crash, tourists had poured into Roswell. And the town had responded. Billing itself as the "UFO Capital of the World," its citizens put up little green men everywhere. Extraterrestrials peeked out from behind fire hydrants and park benches, and

The International UFO Museum and Research Center as it looks today in Roswell, New Mexico.

sat in trees, on lampposts, and in shop windows. A welcome sign shaped like a flying saucer greeted visitors. And restaurants served up "saucer burgers" and "cosmic milkshakes." The town had staged its first UFO festival in the mid-1990s, and thousands of people had descended on Roswell for three days of extraterrestrial food, fun, and games. Already, the town council was planning a celebration for the crash's

179

This humorous sign, complete with flying saucer, little green men, and ordinary folks wearing 1947 clothing, greets visitors to Roswell.

fiftieth anniversary in 1997. It looked to be a blow-out celebration.

Haut hoped his museum—which had opened three years earlier—would become the centerpiece of all the extraterrestrial hoopla. He did face some competition from the UFO Enigma Museum down the street, but he was confident his establishment would prevail.

Strange, then, that while Haut was making money from the flying saucer story, he didn't tell any sensational tales of his own. After all, he'd been an important part of the event. So what were his feelings about UFOs?

Replicas of alien beings abound in Roswell. Here, an extraterrestrial takes in a parking lot.

"I think 99.9 percent of the time such things are explainable," he told a reporter who came to interview him that year.

"Is Roswell the .1 percent?" pressed the reporter.

"Maybe .005 percent," Haut replied.

Haut didn't have much to say about those eventful days in 1947. He claimed not to remember much of anything about the press release. And his wife, he said, didn't recall him coming home that day and mentioning it.

Some ufologists believed Haut was afraid to talk.

Luckily for them, others weren't.

A Roswellian named Jim Ragsdale told ufologists he'd stumbled across the crashed flying saucer while out camping in July of 1947. Not only that, he'd gone inside and pulled the golden helmets right off the alien beings' oversized heads. He'd buried the helmets. Unfortunately, he couldn't remember where.

Lydia Sleppy, who'd worked at an Albuquerque radio station, claimed she was typing up the flying saucer story to send out on the news wires, when the machine she was using suddenly began typing *her* a message. It read: THIS IS THE FBI. YOU WILL IMMEDIATELY CEASE ALL COMMUNICATION. This was a particularly astonishing tale considering the FBI didn't have those sorts of technical capabilities back then.

And Frankie Rowe, who was twelve years old at the time, remembered her father—a Roswell firefighter— being called to the crash site about thirty miles out of town. While there, he saw at least two body bags with something in them. Who, though, would have called the fire department in the first place? Certainly not the military whose officials wanted to keep things "hush-hush." But if Frankie's father saw body bags, then they certainly were already on site. Moreover, none of the other firefighters who'd been in the department at the time remembered going on such a run.

Some UFO researchers took these accounts, and others, seriously. They added them to the core story.

Now, the reconstructed story went like this:

> *In the spring and summer of 1947, saucer-shaped interplanetary spaceships hovered over*

New Mexico. *They wanted to keep track of humankind's scientific progress, and so were drawn to the atomic and rocket research sites there. On July 1, officers at White Sands Proving Ground began tracking these objects. They were recognized as spaceships by their unusual movements. On the evening of July 2, one of these spaceships swooped low over Roswell.*

*On July 4, one of those spaceships malfunctioned, causing it to touch down briefly on Mack Brazel's ranch. It scattered debris, including pieces imprinted with extraterrestrial symbols. The stricken spaceship rose in the air and managed to fly on before crashing into the base of a cliff thirty-five miles north of Roswell.*

*Radar operators at White Sands saw it disappear from their screens. Concluding it had crashed, they searched for it at first light. But the next morning—July 5—before the military could get there, some civilians, including a group of archaeologists, came upon the crash site. Four alien beings were dead, and according to some witnesses, one was alive. They were humanoids, about four feet tall. The military soon arrived. They kicked out the civilians with a warning to stay quiet about what they'd seen. Then under orders from a top-secret group of men called The Nine, they collected the wreckage and the bodies, and cleaned up all traces of the event.*

*The bodies were temporarily taken to the Roswell Army Airfield Hospital, where a civilian witness was ejected by military police and warned not to tell what he'd seen. A redheaded captain also threatened him. All three bodies of alien beings showed signs of exposure to the elements and gave off a terrible odor. The wreckage and bodies were flown to other locations for analysis.*

*That same day, Mack Brazel found the debris on his ranch. But it wasn't until the next day—July 6—that he took some sample debris into town and showed it to Sheriff George Wilcox. Wilcox contacted Roswell Army Air Field and the base intelligence officer, Major*

Jesse Marcel, accompanied by another officer, responded by visiting the ranch with Brazel to collect the material. Among the debris they found lightweight metallic sheets that were harder than anything known on Earth. Troops swept in to collect all the material and remove all traces of the crash.

On July 8, Walter Haut issued a press release announcing the discovery of the remains of a flying saucer. On that same day, the military carefully coached Mack Brazel on a cover story to be given to the press. Thus, the interview published by the Roswell Daily Record was all a lie. Meanwhile, the official press release garnered national attention, but within hours General Roger Ramey denied it. He told the press that the wreckage was merely from a downed weather balloon. He also substituted the extraterrestrial wreckage for authentic bits of weather balloon to fool the press.

Both the press and the public accepted this cover story, concocted to hide the recovery of *a spaceship and extraterrestrial bodies. The government concealed the truth in part to keep the public from panicking. It also considered the find a national security issue. That is, the military wanted to keep secret the advanced scientific knowledge it was gleaning from the spaceship, knowledge that might result in the ultimate secret weapon.*

The Roswell story sure had come a long way from the original, reported events of 1947. From a collection of tinfoil, sticks, and Scotch tape it had grown into a deep-state government cover-up complete with wrecked spaceship and extraterrestrial corpses. But the story wasn't finished yet. What would come next?

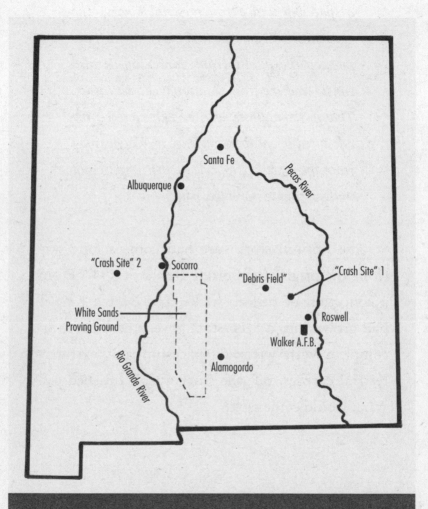

This map shows the locations of the various crash sites.

# ✧ 21 ✧

## An "Alien Autopsy" . . . for Real?

On an August night in 1995, millions of Americans gathered in front of their TV sets to watch a one-hour special called *Alien Autopsy: Fact or Fiction?* The show had been hyped for weeks and promised to show a recently discovered film of the actual autopsy performed on one of the creatures pulled from a flying saucer found near Roswell.

The black-and-white film was grainy, and at times, unfocused. More than once, doctors in full-body HAZMAT suits blocked the cameraman's view. But these flaws only seemed to add to the film's authenticity. So did the tools and medical equipment they used—all vintage 1947.

On an operating table lay a dead space creature—tall, with small, childlike eyes, humanlike ears and mouth, and six fingers. It looked mostly intact except for a large leg wound. As the cameraman focused in, a scalpel cut into the skin along the creature's neck. Dark innards were removed from first its skull, then its abdomen. The gloved hands of the doctors dropped them into pans, and . . .

That was it. The special included just five minutes of the supposedly seventeen-minute-long film.

Could it be real? If so, it shook up everything ufologists had come to acknowledge as the truth about Roswell extraterrestrials. The creature in the film didn't fit the descriptions they'd gathered from witnesses. Could everyone from Stanton Friedman to Donald Schmitt have been wrong? Or was the film a hoax?

It led to hot debate within the UFO community.

Those skeptical of the film wondered why the doctors weren't more careful. Such an extraordinary creature would certainly have been dissected slowly and meticulously. Every step would have been documented. This, after all, would have been an historic autopsy. But no one weighed or labeled the specimens. No one made a photographic record. Those with medical knowledge wondered why, when the organs were removed, there wasn't any connective tissue that required slicing away. Some noticed that the doctors in the film held their scalpels incorrectly.

Those who believed in the film's authenticity responded to these questions. They argued that this had probably been the doctor's third or fourth autopsy, so the procedure had gotten easier. They also argued that the file was obviously old. Just look at it!

In truth, no one had done any conclusive tests on the film. Where had it even come from? The show's producers, Ray Santilli and Gary Shoefield, claimed to have bought it from a retired military cameraman. But they refused to name him . . . for security reasons.

It would be ten years before the truth came out. In 2006, Ray Santilli admitted the film was a fake.

But, he said, it was *based* on the real autopsy of alien beings. He'd seen the real film in its entirety many years earlier, but at the time could not afford to buy it. When he finally did have the money, the original film had grown too old and damaged to use. So he had merely reconstructed the autopsy. "It's no different than restoring a work of art like the *Mona Lisa*," Santilli explained.

As a writer for *Time* magazine noted, that statement could only be true if "restoring the *Mona Lisa* meant painting an entirely new painting of a different woman, on a different canvas, and passing it off as the original."

It was another example of "saucer logic."

# ✧ 22 ✧

## Roswell: Case Closed, or Not?

Colonel John Haynes of the United States Air Force stepped up to the podium. A ripple of laughter ran through the packed room. It wasn't every day that TV and newspaper reporters were summoned to the Pentagon for a press conference about flying saucers. But that's exactly why they'd come on this sunny afternoon in June 1997—to hear the Air Force report on Roswell.

It wasn't the first time officials had publicly answered questions about the incident. Three years earlier, the secretary of the Air Force had directed a search for all records related to Roswell. Any classified information was declassified. Anyone ordered not to talk was released from secrecy. The result of this search had resulted in an in-depth, 800-page analysis titled "The Roswell Report: Fact vs. Fiction in the New Mexico Desert." And in it the Air Force came clean.

They *had* been lying.

There *had* been a cover-up in 1947.

But they hadn't been hiding a flying saucer and its extraterrestrial crew. They'd been hiding Project Mogul.

The military began Project Mogul back in 1946. So secret was the program that even its code name was classified. In those days before satellites and drones, the United States knew little about the Soviet Union's nuclear capabilities. So Mogul's efforts were focused on detecting when the Soviet Union was testing its atomic weapons. In order to hear Soviet blasts, however, sound-detection and data-gathering equipment had to be lifted high into the atmosphere, and suspended there for a long time. This was something ordinary weather balloons could not do. Therefore, Mogul's scientists

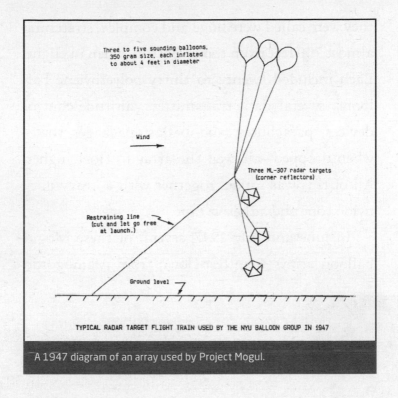

Three to five sounding balloons, 350 gram size, each inflated to about 4 feet in diameter

Wind

Three ML-307 radar targets (corner reflectors)

Restraining line (cut and let go free at launch.)

Ground level

TYPICAL RADAR TARGET FLIGHT TRAIN USED BY THE NYU BALLOON GROUP IN 1947

A 1947 diagram of an array used by Project Mogul.

made their balloons out of a substance never used for that purpose before—polyethylene. Lightweight, and looking much like tin foil, it held its shape and was not easily torn.

Once these special balloons had been created, scientists began launching an odd assortment of sensors and listening devices. These "arrays" as they were called were huge and complex, stretching almost 700 feet from top to bottom when in flight. Each included twenty to thirty polyethylene balloons, several data transmitters, altitude-control devices, parachutes, and ballast packages that—when dropped—allowed the array to float higher. All of this was linked together with a heavy-duty nylon rope and adhesive tape.

In June and July 1947, several of these Mogul balloon arrays were test-flown from Alamogordo

This photo taken in 1948 shows the construction of a Mogul array.

Army Air Base. According to project records, Mogul Flight Four launched on June 4. It flew east toward Roswell, but was struck by lightning during a thunderstorm. It crashed onto Mack Brazel's ranch. On June 14, Brazel found the debris just as he'd originally claimed.

*This*, the Air Force claimed, was what people mistook for flying saucers. *This* was what had scattered

Could this twenty-foot balloon made of polyethylene and used by Project Mogul have been mistaken for a flying saucer? The Air Force believed it was.

debris onto Mack Brazel's ranch. And *this* was why officials had originally lied about it being a regular, old weather balloon. Project Mogul had been top secret.

A seventy-foot-long array is launched.

As for those people like Major Jesse Marcel who claimed they'd never seen anything like this debris, well, they hadn't. Polyethylene balloons were also top secret. Marcel wouldn't have seen one. In fact, the found material—the balsa wood sticks, the reflective tin foils, the parchment paper and rope—all fit the description of a Mogul array.

Even the so-called extraterrestrial writing could be explained. The adhesive tape used by the Mogul scientists had been pink and purple with flowers printed on it. Why? Because that was the tape they'd had on hand, surplus from the war. In fact, many balloon flights—not just Mogul—had also used that flowered tape in the years since then.

The evidence seemed clear, at least to the Air Force—no flying saucers had ever touched down near Roswell.

Given that the military's first words about the incident had been lies, the public was reluctant to let Project Mogul stand as the last word on Roswell. What about the reports of bodies? What about the rumors of autopsies? What about all the military

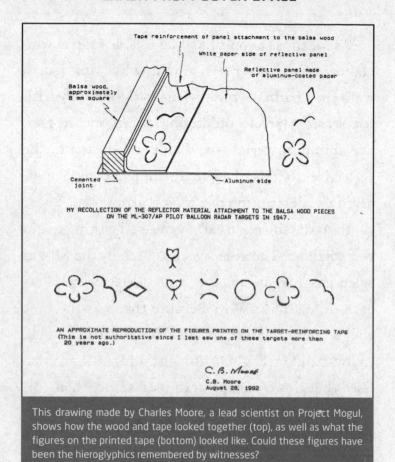

This drawing made by Charles Moore, a lead scientist on Project Mogul, shows how the wood and tape looked together (top), as well as what the figures on the printed tape (bottom) looked like. Could these figures have been the hieroglyphics remembered by witnesses?

personnel, vehicles, and aircraft that reportedly cleaned up the wreckage? The 800-page report barely mentioned any of that. Citizens demanded more information.

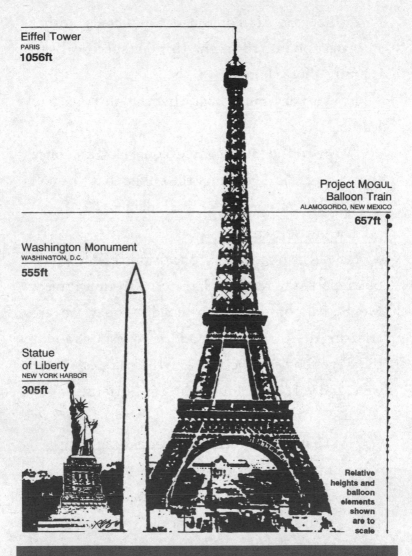

**Eiffel Tower**
PARIS
**1056ft**

**Project MOGUL**
**Balloon Train**
ALAMOGORDO, NEW MEXICO
**657ft**

**Washington Monument**
WASHINGTON, D.C.
**555ft**

**Statue**
**of Liberty**
NEW YORK HARBOR
**305ft**

Relative
heights and
balloon
elements
shown
are to
scale

This chart, created in 1994 by the Air Force, showed just the extraordinary size of a Project Mogul array. With all its shimmering pieces of experimental equipment, it could easily have been misconstrued as a flying saucer.

And so the Air Force had conducted another investigation into the event, this one specifically to examine those claims.

Now, it was time to hear what the Air Force had learned.

"We're confident," began Colonel Haynes, "once the report . . . is digested by the public that this will be the *final* word on the Roswell incident."

The press tittered.

Haynes reiterated the conclusions of the previous report—the remains had come from a Project Mogul balloon—then continued. "Today we are releasing the final report to address questions about the alleged bodies associated with these stories." There were, added Haynes, four main conclusions:

1) That Air Force activities occurring in New Mexico over the course of many years had been consolidated into witnesses' memories, meaning, they'd taken separate events that had happened, perhaps over decades, and

compressed them into two or three days in July 1947. "As we age, we not only begin to confuse the years, but also the decades," Haynes said.

2) The bodies seen were "probably test dummies that were carried aloft by . . . high altitude balloons for scientific research." Scientists had just begun using test dummies in 1947, so the public would not have been familiar with them at the time. They would have been easily mistaken for real people . . . or alien beings.

3) The unusual military activity in the desert was "high altitude research balloon launch and recovery operations." Here his voice took on a sarcastic tone. "Reports of the military units that always seemed to arrive shortly after a crash were actually accurate . . ." They weren't, however, there

to pick up a flying saucer, but rather a downed, highly secret balloon and accompanying test dummies.

4) Claims of extraterrestrial bodies at Roswell Army Air Field hospital were "most likely a combination of two separate incidents." The first was a 1956 aircraft accident in which eleven airmen lost their lives. The second was a 1959 manned balloon mishap in which an airman was injured. Once again, this was a case of faulty memory and time compression.

Haynes then showed film footage from the archives of the Defense Department, showing balloon flights, experiments with dummies, and other equipment launched into the air, including Project Mogul.

The press laughed sheepishly through this part. *All* the footage looked like flying saucers

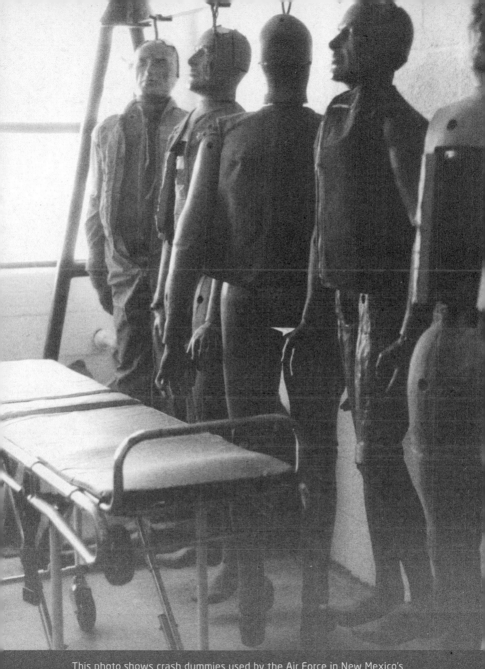

This photo shows crash dummies used by the Air Force in New Mexico's desert. Could these have been mistaken for alien beings?

In this photo shown at the 1997 press conference, an aeroshell used in the 1960s to test the parachutes for the NASA Viking Mars Program is being prepared to be lifted high into the atmosphere by a balloon. Its likeness to a flying saucer made reporters laugh self-consciously.

This photo, also shown to reporters at the 1997 press conference, shows the aeroshell after it had detached from the balloon and descended back to earth. Reporters laughed heartily at what appeared to be an upside-down flying saucer.

or UFOs. How silly to have mistaken them for extraterrestrials.

Many ufologists, however, met this report with skepticism. The Air Force's answers felt too pat, too tidy. Why hadn't anyone mentioned test dummies earlier? And, come on, did the Air Force truly believe faulty memory and time compression explained it

207

all away? Despite the report's title, "The Roswell Report: Case Closed," it was anything but.

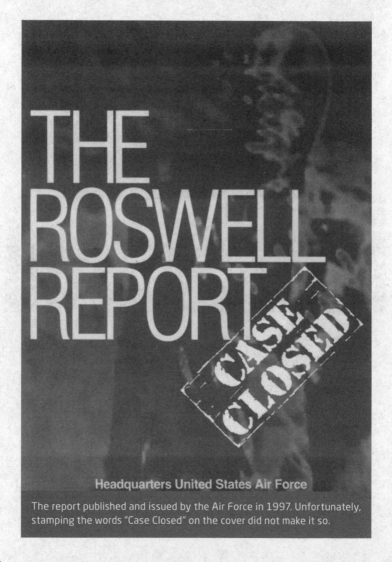

The report published and issued by the Air Force in 1997. Unfortunately, stamping the words "Case Closed" on the cover did not make it so.

## ✧ 23 ✧

## Why, Frank, Why?

Throughout the 1990s, Frank Kaufmann continued to feed ufologists stories about extraterrestrials, cover-ups, and The Group of Nine. He kept hinting about the cache of documents in his home office—evidence that proved he spoke the truth. He would hand them over when the time was right, he repeatedly said. Sadly, that time never came. In February 2001, Kaufmann passed away.

Eager to get Kaufmann's documentary evidence, ufologists asked his wife for access to his papers. She agreed. In his office, they opened drawers and files.

And they discovered a dark secret.

In a cabinet they found a stack of blank, World War II-era stationary. And on a table behind his desk, they found a typewriter from the same time period. They typed a few words on the machine and compared them to the documents he'd shown them. The type matched exactly.

Kaufmann had fabricated it all. He'd counterfeited every document.

Why?

No one, not even his wife, knew the answer.

The truth was a punch to Kevin Randle's gut. Blips on a radar screen. The location of the crash site. A deep-state cover-up overseen by The Group of Nine. None of it was real. And the Roswell reconstruction he'd based on Kauffman's testimony? It was nothing but a fairy tale.

## ❖ 24 ❖

# A Case of Wishful Thinking?

Donald Schmitt and his new partner, Tom Carey, were feeling desperate. After years of Roswell research, they still hadn't turned up any physical proof of an extraterrestrial crash. And time was running out. With nothing concrete to link Brazel's debris to extraterrestrials, Roswell was becoming a cold case. The ufologists needed new and conclusive evidence . . . soon.

In 2012, Tom Carey received a phone call from a businessman named Joseph Beason. Earlier that year, Beason had obtained a collection of photographic slides reportedly taken during the 1940s by a well-to-do Texas couple, the late Bernard and

Hilda Ray. Two of the slides were especially interesting. They seemed to show a tiny, dead body resting on a glass shelf. Beason thought it looked like an extraterrestrial. Could Carey and Schmitt authenticate the photos?

Carey agreed to take a look. Soon afterward, Beason emailed him a scan of one of the slides. The UFO researcher clicked it open . . . and sat bolt upright. The image showed a small, brown withered body in a glass case. The figure had a large triangle-shaped skull with elongated eye sockets and a tiny slit of a mouth. But it was the mark on the figure's head that particularly fascinated Carey. He'd seen this dark indentation before, on a desert insect called "el Niño de la Tierra,"—"the child of the Earth."

Carey's thoughts whirled. According to one Roswell witness, her father had seen three dead extraterrestrials at the crash site. When she'd urged him to describe the creatures, he'd responded "child of earth."

This description had long puzzled Carey. But now came a revelation. "When I saw that image . . . it jumped right at me. That's what [her father] was talking about," Carey later explained. "Also, the body looked exactly like what had been described to me by several eyewitnesses . . . My first thought was: this has to be one of the Roswell bodies . . . and [the photo] was taken right after recovery."

He and Schmitt had the slides investigated by the best photographic experts, who confirmed they'd been taken between 1945 and 1950. Experts also examined the cardboard mountings around the slides, verifying that the slides had been developed around that time, too.

Thrilled by the results, the ufologists looked into the lives of Bernard and Hilda Ray. Bernard, they learned, had been a geologist. Could the couple have been out rock hunting in the area the day of the crash? Midland Texas, their hometown, was just 250 miles from Roswell. As for Hilda, she'd been a lawyer and had a pilot's license—unconventional activities for a woman in those days. Carey suspected she was involved with intelligence during World War II. He suspected the couple were friends of President and Mamie Eisenhower, too.

Carey sent a copy of one of the slides to an old associate, Richard Doble, a physical anthropologist at the University of Toronto. Doble was startled by what he saw. "It's nothing like [humans], we can see that his feet and legs appear to be like that of a reptile . . . His nose is small, his mouth different from ours. There are parts that could have been removed during autopsy. [It] seems to have no teeth . . . The more you look at it, the more you realize it is not from earth."

He also showed the slide to an Air Force veteran who claimed he'd seen the corpses being brought into the base hospital at Roswell. "That's what I saw in 1947," he confirmed.

Meanwhile, rumors of the slides rippled through the UFO community. Had Schmitt and Carey finally found proof positive of an extraterrestrial crash? If so, why weren't they talking about it?

In truth, neither ufologist wanted to say anything until they'd positively verified the photo. Too many times UFO researchers had fallen for hoaxes—Frank Kaufmann, Glenn Dennis, the M-12 Documents among them. No, they wanted to be certain.

Finally, in November 2014, Carey couldn't keep quiet any longer. "We have the smoking gun!" he blurted out during a UFO conference in Washington, DC. "The slides are from 1947 . . . and [they] show an [extraterrestrial] who's been partially dissected lying in a case."

The audience buzzed. The slides, if real, confirmed the most sensational aspect of the Roswell story—the autopsies of alien bodies.

The press buzzed, too. The story was the lead on television news shows. It made the front pages of magazines and newspapers. "It certainly is the most important event of our lifetimes," Schmitt told reporters.

A date was set to reveal the slides: May 5, 2015, in Mexico City. And a big extravaganza, called BeWitness, was planned. Nearly 7,000 people paid between $20 and $86 to attend the event, and thousands more from all around the world paid $20 to watch the livestream. The reveal event began with a presentation by Carey and Schmitt. The spectacle, which lasted four hours, featured a long list of speakers, including a costumed actor dressed as an extraterrestrial. The evening's highlight, however, was Carey and Schmitt's presentation. They detailed their investigation, as well as their conclusion. Anthropologist Richard Doble added to the presentation by testifying that the body was not human.

Then, at long last, the two slides were projected onto enormous screens.

The crowd seemed at a loss for words. They appeared stunned at the mysterious figure illuminated before them. Was this real? Was the world finally going to learn the truth about alien beings?

Schmitt and Carey expected accolades. But at first there was little response from the UFO world. A blurry image of both slides was on the Internet. But they were so hard to see. Was that a placard on the shelf next to the alien body? Why would a top secret dead extraterrestrial need a placard? It had writing on it, but it was indecipherable. Had Schmitt and Carey tried to read it?

Carey responded: "We've had everyone . . . even the Photo Interpretation Department of the Pentagon, as well as Adobe [all tell us] it's beyond the pale, that it cannot be read, it's totally up to interpretation."

Obviously, Carey and Schmitt interpreted it as reading "extraterrestrial."

Meanwhile, a group of independent UFO researchers calling themselves the Roswell Slides Research Group (RSRG) began their own investigation. They started with the placard. If only they could read it. Luckily, someone involved in the slide-reveal show leaked them a high-resolution image.

A member of the RSRG quickly used the commercial software app SmartDeblur to read the placard. Its first line read: MUMMIFIED BODY OF TWO YEAR OLD BOY.

Online, the UFO community buzzed. Hooted one researcher, "You folks solved in no more than 2 or 3 days what the promoters claimed not to have solved in 3 years!"

Carey and Schmitt were furious. They accused the RSRG of Photoshopping the placard.

But further deblurring revealed the rest of the placard: "At the time of burial the body was clothing in a (unreadable) cotton shirt. Burial wrappings consisted of these small cotton blankets. Loaned by Mr. (unreadable) San Francisco, California."

Still, Carey and Schmitt clung to their belief in the photos.

But the information kept coming. A better reading of the placard revealed the donor's name: S. L. Palmer. Other online researchers located government records showing Palmer had found the child's mummy in 1896 near Montezuma Castle, a series of caves in Arizona. They traced the mummy—that of an Indigenous American child—to Mesa Verde Archeological Museum in Mesa Verde, Colorado. Documents showed it had been displayed between 1938 and June 1947. This was probably where the Rays took their photos. Later, curators sent the mummy to Montezuma Castle National Monument Museum in Camp Verde, Arizona, where it remained on exhibit throughout the 1950s.

Schmitt threw in the towel. He claimed he'd been "overly trusting."

Carey, however, insisted the matter was "still open to debate."

Many UFO researchers felt deeply embarrassed by the episode. Not only had the credibility of Roswell research been damaged, but ufology in general. "It's the biggest black eye," said one researcher.

The slide incident did not end the search for proof of a Roswell saucer crash. But it did convince many researchers to look elsewhere for encounters with alien beings.

"Our revels here have ended," wrote Karl Pflock. "Time now to pursue other hopes and dreams with our feet firmly planted on the ground and our eyes on the skies—taking great care where we step."

# PART 4

## Who Knows What the Government Knows?

## ✧ **25** ✧

## Why So Secretive?

Buried deep in the Pentagon building's maze of hallways lurked a shadowy program: the Advanced Aerospace Threat Identification Program (AAITP). Few knew its purpose. Fewer still knew it existed.

Luis Elizondo, the intelligence officer who oversaw the program, liked it that way. Secrecy made his job—investigating the UFOs that had been seen buzzing US military jets, ships, and installations—much easier. Did they threaten national security?

When he'd first been offered the job in 2007, Elizondo had been asked what he thought of UFOs. "I don't think much about them at all," he

An aerial view of the Pentagon building in Washington, DC. Hidden somewhere in this vast maze was the office of the Advanced Aerospace Threat Identification Program.

replied. It was the right answer. But what he learned over the next ten years convinced him that UFOs needed to be taken seriously. One incident in particular shook him.

In November 2004, the Nimitz Carrier Strike Group, an assemblage of navy cruisers and aircraft carriers, headed out to the restricted waters off the coast of San Diego and Baja, California, to conduct training operations. Suddenly, the advance radar on one of the ships, the USS *Princeton*, began registering some strange presences. They were logged flying as high as 80,000 feet, and as low as the ocean's surface. These extraordinary radar observations continued for a full week.

Finally, Commander David Fravor of the Black Aces Squadron was sent up to intercept the presence. As he soared to the object's location in his fighter jet, he looked down and saw an oval-shaped craft, about the size of a commercial airplane, hovering over the waves. It didn't have wings, or any other obvious flight surfaces, and Fravor could not identify any means of propulsion. The object bounced around like a Ping-Pong ball. Two other pilots, one seated behind him, and another in a nearby plane, saw the same thing. Fravor descended, intending to chase the object. But it zipped away at an incredible speed.

Another pilot, Chad Underwood, was also sent up. Via the camera on his jet's left wing, he recorded a video of the object. The one-minute, sixteen-second clip showed a blurry, dark dot against a gray background. In the video's last second, the object seemed to outwit the jet, darting away.

"It was behaving in ways that aren't physically normal," recalled Underwood. "Aircraft, whether they're manned or unmanned, still have to obey the laws of physics."

It was cases like this, and dozens of others, that convinced Elizondo that UFOs posed a threat to national security. He urged the Department of Defense to take them seriously. After all, he told officials, he wasn't talking about little green men here. He was talking about objects that had been seen by Navy and Air Force pilots or had been picked up by satellite imagery. These objects engaged in actions that were hard to explain; movements that were hard to replicate. They possessed technology unknown to humans and traveled faster than the speed of sound. Why didn't the military seem to care?

Elizondo kept trying to convey his concerns to higher-ups in the Pentagon's chain of command. Unidentified flying objects, or as the military now called them, Unidentified Aerial Phenomena (UAPs) were threats. Take the USS *Theodore Roosevelt* incident.

In late 2014 and early 2015, Super Hornets attached to the *Roosevelt* off the eastern seaboard near Florida began encountering fast-moving, unidentified aircraft that looked like, in one pilot's words, "a cube encasing a sphere." The warplanes tracked these strange targets with their upgraded radar. The planes' video cameras also captured the objects.

"They're all going against the wind," marveled one pilot in a recorded encounter. "The wind's one hundred twenty knots to the west."

"Look at that thing, dude!" cried another pilot. "Look at that thing! It's rotating!"

Later, one of the pilots claimed the objects reacted to the planes and moved around them.

Others asserted these objects traveled five times the speed of sound and stayed in the air for up to twelve hours without refueling. Some of the objects descended into the water, as shown on videos taken by Navy personnel.

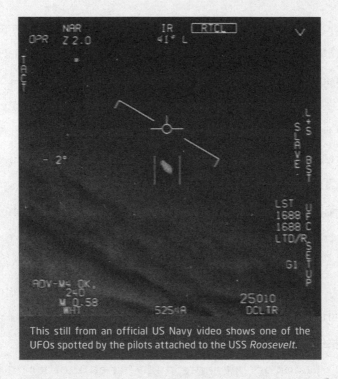

This still from an official US Navy video shows one of the UFOs spotted by the pilots attached to the USS *Roosevelt*.

The fact that these UAPs appeared near American aircraft carriers should have worried the military. And in fact, officials *did* brief the Senate Armed Services Committee about the sightings. And then? Nothing.

In October 2017, frustrated at the military's lack of response, Elizondo resigned from his position. He'd decided to take his concerns directly to the American public.

He spoke with *New York Times* reporters about his secret activities. The article, published in December 2017, drew thousands of readers, and appeared on major news channels. In a few short weeks, a topic long confined to tabloids and fringe media became a serious news story. If the military was investigating UAPs, there *must* be something to them.

It was the public's renewed fascination with UAPs that spurred the Pentagon to beef up their investigations into unusual sightings. Said one official in 2019, "The UAP issue is being taken very seriously now even compared to where it was two or three years ago."

That same year, the Navy revised its guidelines for pilots. Once, service members claiming to see UAPs had been ridiculed, or even reprimanded. Now, top brass encouraged them to report sightings.

In September, a Navy spokesman announced that the videos from pilot Chad Underwood's camera, along with videos of those 2014–2015 sightings showed "incursions into our military training ranges by unidentified flying phenomenon." When some reporters noted that the videos looked like nothing more than blurry dots, the spokesman responded by pointing out that there was far more "classified" material on the sightings.

Those who remembered the days of Project Blue Book saw this as a huge change. This time, the military wasn't acting as if nothing had happened. It wasn't assigning a logical explanation. Instead, it was admitting there was more to the incidents. It was saying there were things in the sky they couldn't identify.

Changes came fast now.

In August 2020, the Department of Defense announced the creation of the Unidentified Aerial Phenomena Task Force. Its mission was to "detect, analyze and catalog UAPs that could cause a threat to national security." Its first order of business? Submit a report to Congress about national security investigations of unidentified aerial phenomena.

The public eagerly waited for this report, especially ufologists. Since the days of Donald Keyhoe and NICAP, they'd been hoping for disclosure.

Could it be that the government would finally come clean and confess all their UFO secrets?

Did they have spaceships hidden away?

What about the bodies of alien beings?

Had a flying saucer crashed at Roswell?

# ✧ 26 ✧

## The Truth?

The long-awaited report arrived on June 25, 2021. It was just nine pages long.

And while the UAP Task Force did provide some new information, it left many of the biggest questions unanswered.

Yes, Navy pilots and other military personnel had being seen mysterious flying objects for years. A Navy task force had reviewed 144 sightings by service members between 2004 and 2021.

Of those 144 sightings, they could only determine an explanation for one—a deflating balloon.

In eighteen of the cases, military personnel reported advanced, as-of-yet unknown technological capabilities.

In eleven instances, pilots reported dangerous "near misses" with UAP.

So what did the task force conclude?

The objects were not part of a secret US weapons program, said the report. Additionally, they most likely were physical objects, since they had been detected in multiple ways: "radar, infra-red, weapon seekers and visual observation." They clearly posed a threat to civilian flight safety, as well as "pose[d] a challenge" to national security. And finally, the government needed to collect and analyze more information, as well as develop a way to screen and process UAP reports.

What did the report say about alien beings?

Nothing.

It didn't mention interplanetary travel or extraterrestrial life once. And it never implied that alien beings from space had sent the UAPs.

The UFO community was deeply disappointed.

On May 17, 2021, former President Barack Obama appeared on *The Late Late Show with James Corden*. He was asked what he knew about extraterrestrials. He replied:

"Look, the truth is, when I came into office, I asked, 'Is there a lab somewhere we're keeping [extraterrestrial] specimens and a spaceship?' They did a little bit of research, and the answer was no. But what is true—and I'm actually being serious—is that there's footage and records of objects in the skies that we don't know exactly what they are. We can't explain how they moved, their trajectory, they did not have an easily explainable pattern. I think that people still take seriously trying to investigate and figure out what that is."

People *are* still investigating.

They *are* still taking it seriously.

There is so much more that remains unknown.

Did something crash from outer space?

You decide.

# ☆ AUTHOR'S NOTE ☆

What a weird journey this book has taken me on. In the course of my research, I've hunted for spaceship crash sites in the New Mexico desert, learned from a real-life UFO investigator how to track extraterrestrial encounters, and spent long hours peering at grainy home movies of mysterious lights and blinking orbs. Who says research isn't fun?

It all began with immersion in the vast files of the J. Allen Hynek Center for UFO Studies (CUFOS). CUFOS is dedicated to serious academic and scientific study of UFO activity. It maintains a library and archive of UFO-related materials, as well as investigates UFO sightings, collecting and evaluating reports. Its files overflow with contemporary accounts of Roswell, as well as scholarly and up-to-date articles about the event. Kenneth

Arnold's flying crescent sighting can also be found in the archive, as well and thousands of other sightings and encounters. Sadly, CUFOS no longer has a physical location. But it has made its archive of 70,000 documents available online. It's an incredible trove.

Through CUFOS I got to know its director, Dr. Mark Rodeghier, who not only explained how the day-to-day business of investigating UFOs is done (interviews, gathering of evidence, and double-checking findings), but he also provided fascinating insight into his studies on waves of UFO sightings and the changes in UFO report characteristics. From him I gained a real sense of the work done by Edward Ruppelt and Allen Hynek so many years ago. I also acquired a deeper understanding of ufologists—their passion and persistence.

Because of another online archive—mysteriously called The Black Vault—I was able to dig through more than 10,000 declassified government documents pertaining to the top secret Project Blue Book. Thanks to UFO enthusiast John Greenewald Jr. it is all there. And I mean *all*. The site boasts 2.2 million documents, and contains every single instance of UFO sightings stored in US government files. *Wowsa!*

My research journey also took me to the Mutual UFO Network (MUFON). MUFON is an international organization dedicated to using scientific procedures and techniques to study UFO phenomena. I was delighted to discover that MUFON has local chapters that sponsor "meetups"—the modern-day equivalent of those long-ago flying saucer clubs. Over coffee at a local diner, members chat about recent sightings and consider evidence. But they do it with a twenty-first-century twist. MUFON members have a working knowledge of weather patterns and astronomy. They also have access to an online tool that allows them to check local air traffic to determine if a sighting was actually an airplane. As if that isn't enough, they also have online image analysis tools to help gauge the authenticity of photographs, as well as a huge and detailed "case management system" that members can tap into to research past sightings and other UFO-related events. But my favorite MUFON tool is the "UFO Stalker." With just a couple computer clicks, members can see where in the world UFOs have been sighted. They can read the case reports, and look at any available photos or video. Best of all, UFO Stalker is updated daily. So every morning as a member (and yes, research led me to become a member) I can look to see if anyone in my neighborhood has seen something weird in the skies. So far, they haven't. But I'm still checking.

Of course, my research journey led me to Roswell . . . twice! At the International UFO Museum and Research Center, I read yellowing firsthand accounts of so-called witnesses, and took in the cheesy dioramas of saucer crashes and extraterrestrial autopsies. I strolled past the Ballard Funeral Home where Glenn Dennis once worked, and drove the five miles out to the Roswell Air Center, once the Roswell Army Air Force Base. I tried to imagine the town as it looked in 1947, before it became the "UFO Capital of the World." Then I headed out into the desert to search for crash sites. Three different crash sites have been popularized over the years by various ufologists, writers, and filmmakers. But one particular plot of land seventy-five miles from Roswell is said to be the spot where the flying saucer with its spaceman crew finally landed. It's hard to get to, and on private property. There isn't any cell service, and one has to keep an eye out for rattlesnakes and tarantulas. A rough and rutted dirt path leads to a rusted-out truck and a wooden shed. This is the debris field, but any evidence is long gone. Not a scrap of foil-like metal or bit of flowered tape remains. There is just earth and sky and a granite stone marking the spot.

Research is often a team sport. I didn't trek across the desert alone. Eric Rohmann, as well as Paul and Katrin Tiernan, gamely came along, clambering over rocks and arroyos, and declaring it all fun.

No, I may not have found a flying saucer crash site. But I *did* uncover a terrific story. And every word of it is true.

# ☆ BIBLIOGRAPHY ☆

## PRIMARY SOURCES
### Books

Arnold, Kenneth, and Ray Palmer. *The Coming of the Saucers*. Amherst, WI: Privately Published, 1952.

Hynek, J. Allen. *The Hynek UFO Report*. New York: Barnes & Noble Books, 1997.

——. *The Hynek UFO Report: The Authoritative Account of the Project Blue Book Cover-Up*. Newburyport, MA: MUFON, 2020.

Keyhoe, Donald. *The Flying Saucers Are Real*. New York: Fawcett Publications, 1950.

——. *The Flying Saucer Conspiracy*. New York: Holt, Rinehart and Winston, 1955.

Maday, Henry, John E. L. Tenney, and Laura Marxer. *The Vimana: Classic UFO Collection 1954–1955; Official Publication of the Detroit Saucer Club*. Scotts Valley, CA: CreateSpace Independent Publishing Platform, 2018.

Ruppelt, Edward J. *The Report on Unidentified Flying Objects*. New York: Doubleday & Company Inc., 1956.

——. The Report on Unidentified Flying Objects. 2nd expanded edition. New York: Ballantine, 1960.

Scully, Frank. *Behind the Flying Saucers*. New York: Henry Holt and Company, 1950.

## Magazine and Newspaper Articles

Cahn, J. P. "The Flying Saucers and the Mysterious Little Men." *True*, September 1952.

Darrach, H.B. Jr., and Robert Ginna. "Have We Visitors from Space?" *Life*, April 7, 1952.

"Harassed Rancher Who Located 'Saucer' Sorry He Told About It." *Roswell Daily Record*, July 9, 1947.

Keyhoe, Donald. "The Flying Saucers Are Real." *True*, May 1949.

"Roswell Hardware Man and Wife Report Disk Seen." *Roswell Daily Record*, July 8, 1947.

"Roswell Statement." *San Francisco Chronicle*, July 9, 1947.

Severson, Thor. "Here's Latest in 'Saucers.'" *Lethbridge Herald*, March 24, 1950.

## Other Documents and Videos

C–SPAN. "Air Force Report on Roswell Events."
C–SPAN.org. https://www.c-span.org/video/?87217-1/
air-force-report-roswell-events.

Federal Bureau of Investigation. "Majestic 12." FBI
Records: The Vault. https://vault.fbi.gov/
Majestic%2012.

Office of the Director of National Intelligence.
"Preliminary Assessment: Unidentified Aerial
Phenomena." dni.gov. https://www.dni.gov/
files/ODNI/documents/assessments/Preliminary-
Assessment-UAP-20210625.pdf.

The Late Late Show with James Corden. "Obama Talks
UFOs on James Corden." YouTube.com. https://
www.youtube.com/watch?v=tKSyYTerGTI.

US Department of Defense. "Statement by
Department of Defense on the Release of Historic
Navy Videos." defense.gov. https://www.defense.
gov/News/Releases/Release/Article/2165713/
statement-by-the-department-of-defense-on-the-
release-of-historical-navy-videos/.

US National Archives. "Interview of Gerald Anderson 07/
24/1991." YouTube.com. https://www.youtube.com/
watch?v=ivaWnbKsBkM.

## SECONDARY SOURCES
### Books

Berliner, Don, and Stanton T. Friedman. *Crash at Corona*. New York: Marlowe & Company, 1992.

Berlitz, Charles, and William L. Moore. *The Roswell Incident*. New York: Grossett & Dunlap, 1980.

Bloecher, Ted. *Report on the UFO Wave of 1947*. Washington, DC: National Investigation Committee on Aerial Phenomena, 1967.

Hogan, David J. *UFO FAQ: All That's Left to Know About Roswell, Aliens, Whirling Discs, and Flying Saucers*, Milwaukee: Backbeat Books, 2016.

Jacobsen, Annie. *Area 51: An Uncensored History of America's Top Secret Military Base*. New York: Back Bay Books, 2011.

McAndrews, James. *The Roswell Report: Fact vs. Fiction in the New Mexico Desert*. Washington, DC: United States Government Printing Office, 1995.

Moseley, James W., and Karl T. Pflock. *Shockingly Close to the Truth: Confessions of a Grave-Robbing Ufologist.* Amherst, NY: Prometheus Books, 2002.

Pflock, Karl T. *Roswell: Inconvenient Facts and the Will to Believe.* Amherst, NY: Prometheus Books, 2001.

Randle, Kevin D. *Crash: When UFOs Fall From The Sky: A History of Famous Incidents, Conspiracies, and Cover-Ups.* Franklin Lakes, NJ: New Page Books, 2010.

Randle, Kevin D., and Donald R. Schmitt. *The Truth about the UFO Crash at Roswell.* New York: M. Evans & Co., 1994.

Sagan, Carl. *The Demon Haunted World: Science as a Candle in the Dark.* New York: Ballantine Books, 1996.

## Magazines and Journal Articles

Carlson, Peter. "50 Years Ago, Unidentified Flying Objects From Way Beyond the Beltway Seized the Capital's Imagination." *Washington Post,* July 21, 2002. https://www.washingtonpost.com/archive/lifestyle/2002/07/21/50-years-ago-unidentified-flying-objects-from-way-beyond-the-beltway-seized-the-capitals-imagination/59f74156-51f4-4204-96df-e12be061d3f8/.

Carpenter, Les. "The Curious Case of the Alien in the Photo and the Mystery That Took Years to Solve." *Guardian*, September 30, 2017. https//the guardian .com/science/2017/Sep/30/alien-photo-Rosewell-new-mexico-mystery.

Cooper, Helen, Ralph Blumenthal, and Leslie Kean. "'Wow, What Is That?' Navy Pilots Report Unexplained Flying Objects." *New York Times*, May 27, 2019.

David, Leonard. "Experts Weigh In on Pentagon UFO Report." *Scientific American*, June 8, 2021. scientificamerican.com/article/experts-weigh-in-on-pentagon-ufo-report/.

Eichstaedt, Peter. "The Crash at Roswell: A Lingering Mystery." *New Mexico Magazine*, November 1994.

Goldstein, Laurence. "The Reality of Flying Saucers." *The Baltimore Sun*, May 31, 1992, 3H.

Kloor, Keith. "UFOs Won't Go Away." *Issues in Science and Technology* 35, no. 3, Spring 2019. https:// issues.org/ufos-wont-go-away/.

Lagerfeld, Nathalie. "How an Alien Autopsy Hoax Captured the World's Imagination for a Decade."

*Time*, June 24, 2016. https://time.com/4376871/
alien-autopsy-hoax-history/.

Lewis-Krause, Gideon. "How the Pentagon Started
Taking U.F.O.S Seriously." *New Yorker*, April 30,
2021. newyorker.com/magazine/2021/05/10/how-
the-pentagon-started-taking-ufos-seriously?source=
search_google_dsa_paid&gclid=Cj0KCQjwt-
6LBhDlARIsAIPRQcIKPLg57FgiPFuYccf
Y6phQUqiyYbHuZv-vtGwGQrVFIvrmNHtCX-
MaAjzREALw_wcB.

McCarthy, Paul. "The Case of the Missing Nurses."
*Omni,* Fall 1995.

Pflock, Karl T. "Star Witness: The Mortician of Roswell
Breaks His Code of Silence." *Omni*, Fall 1995.

Randle, Kevin D., and Mark Rodeghier. "Frank
Kaufmann Reconsidered." *IUR*, Fall 2002.

Shatz, Itamar. "The Sagan Standard: Extraordinary
Claims Require Extraordinary Evidence."
Effectiviology. com. https://effectiviology.com/
sagan-standard-extraordinary-claims-require-
extraordinary-evidence/.

Sheaffer, Robert. "The 'Roswell Slides' Fiasco: Ufology's Biggest Black Eye." *Skeptical Inquirer*, September/October 2015.

Tangermann, Victor. "Navy Pilot Describes Bizzare 'Tic Tac' UFO Encounter He Filmed." Futurism.com. https://futurism.com/ navy-pilot-bizzare-ufo-encounter.

# ☆ SOURCE NOTES ☆

## Chapter 3: What Could It Be?

"mirror reflecting sunlight . . .": Ted Bloecher, *Report on the UFO Wave of 1947* (Washington, DC: National Investigation Committee on Aerial Phenomena, 1967), I–1.

"the tail of a kite": ibid.

"an eerie feeling": Kenneth Arnold and Ray Palmer, *The Coming of the Saucers* (Amherst, WI: Privately Published, 1952), 6.

"like a saucer . . .": Edward J. Ruppelt, *The Report On Unidentified Flying Objects* (New York: Doubleday & Company, Inc., 1956), 5.

## Chapter 4: Could It *Really* Be a Flying Saucer?

"quite a bit of debris": James McAndrews, *The Roswell Report: Fact vs. Fiction in the New Mexico Desert* (Washington, DC: United States Government Printing Office, 1995), Appendix 1.

"He couldn't cut it . . .": Peter Eichstaedt, "The Crash at Roswell: A Lingering Mystery," *New Mexico Magazine*, November 1994, 29.

"three quarters of a mile . . .": Karl T. Pflock, *Roswell: Inconvenient Facts and the Will to Believe* (Amherst, NY: Prometheus Books, 2001), 92.

"It was something . . .": ibid.

"no fresh impact . . .": ibid.

"They tried to make . . .": "Harassed Rancher Who Located 'Saucer' Sorry He Told About It," *Roswell Daily Record*, July 9, 1947, 1.

"When [it] was all gathered . . .": ibid.

## Chapter 5: Is Anyone Telling the Truth?

"The many rumors . . .": "Roswell Statement," *San Francisco Chronicle*, July 9, 1947, 1.

"They were quite . . .": Dava Sobel, "The Truth About Roswell," *Omni*, Fall 1995, 98.

"shut up": Charles Berlitz and William L. Moore, *The Roswell Incident* (New York: Grosset & Dunlap, 1980), 35.

"Maybe forty or fifty . . .": Pflock, *Roswell: Inconvenient Facts*, 27.

"As far as I can . . .": "Roswell Statement," 1.

"rather tough paper": "Harassed Rancher," 1.

"tape with flowers . . .": ibid.

"I am sure . . .": ibid.

## Chapter 6: Little Green Men from Venus . . . Really?

"lines of magnetic force": Frank Scully, *Behind the Flying Saucers* (New York: Henry Holt and Company, 1950), 25.

"virtually unlimited": Thor Severson, "Here's Latest in 'Saucers,'" *Lethbridge Herald*, March 24, 1950, 6.

"if the earth's gauge . . .": ibid.

"little men": ibid.

"It disappeared": ibid.

"indestructible [extraterrestrial] material": ibid.

"electrifying" and "spellbinding": Scully., 5.

"absurd" and "unbelievable": ibid.

"valuable information": ibid.

"Did the speaker . . .": Severson, 6.

"Was he an expert . . .": ibid.

"Had the information . . .": ibid.

## Chapter 7: Can It Be True?

"What are flying saucers . . .": Scully, book cover.

## Chapter 8: Who Are These Mysterious Little Men?

"For four months . . .": J. P. Cahn, "The Flying Saucers and the Mysterious Little Men," *True*, September 1952, 17.

"headed up 1,700 scientists . . .": Scully, 41.

"I learned that two men . . .": Cahn, 36.

"And what you can't prove . . .": ibid., 112.

## Chapter 9: Saucers over the White House?

"Here's a fleet . . .": Peter Carlson, "50 Years Ago, Unidentified Flying Objects From Way Beyond the Beltway Seized the Capital's Imagination," *Washington Post*, July 21, 2002, https://www.washingtonpost.com/archive/lifestyle/2002/07/21/50-years-ago-unidentified-flying-objects-from-way-beyond-the-beltway-seized-the-capitals-imagination/59f74156-51f4-4204-96df-e12be061d3f8/.

"an orange ball . . .": ibid.

"like falling stars . . .": ibid.

"I was at my maximum . . .": ibid.

"Saucers Swarm Over Capital": ibid.

"Jets Chase D.C. Sky Ghost": ibid.

## Chapter 10: Does the Air Force Believe in UFOS . . . or Doesn't It?

"draw a picture. . .": Ruppelt, 140.

"What was the condition . . ." ibid.

"out of patriotic duty": Donald Keyhoe, *The Flying Saucers Are Real* (New York: Fawcett Publications, 1950), 162.

"just a lot of nonsense": J. Allen Hynek, *The Hynek UFO Report* (New York: Barnes & Noble Books, 1997), 7.

"figments of the imagination": ibid., 23.

"I enjoyed the role . . .": ibid., 7.

"like a mother craft . . .": H. B. Darrach Jr. and Robert Ginna, "Have We Visitors From Space?" *Life*, April 7, 1952, 82.

"fighting City Hall": Hynek, 35.

"UFO phenomena is real . . .": ibid., 17.

## Chapter 11: Who Is Watching the Skies?

"saucerian conversation": Henry Maday, John E. L. Tenney, and Laura Marxer, *The Vimana: Classic UFO Collection 1954–1955; Official Publication of the Detroit Saucer Club* (Scotts Valley, CA: CreateSpace Independent Publishing Platform, 2018), 47.

"Keep watching the skies:" Laurence Goldstein, "The Reality of Flying Saucers," The *Baltimore Sun*, May 31, 1992, 3H.

"We have survived . . .". Donald Keyhole, "The Flying Saucers Are Real," *True*, May 1949, 17.

Will no one tell . . .": Donald Keyhole, *The Flying Saucer Conspiracy* (New York: Holt, Rinehart and Winston, 1955), 6.

"saucer problem": ibid., 8.

"Extraterrestrials must be convinced . . .": ibid., 28.

"saucer screwball": Edward J. Ruppelt, *The Report On Unidentified Flying Objects*, 2nd expanded edition (New York: Ballantine, 1960), 301.

"It isn't the UFOs . . .": ibid.

"Certainly, a careful . . .": J. Allen Hynek, *The Hynek UFO Report: The Authoritative Account of the Project Blue Book Cover-Up* (Newburyport, MA: MUFON, 2020), 2.

## Chapter 13: Did You *Personally* See a Crashed Flying Saucer?

"[We] went after the story . . .": Annie Jacobsen, *Area 51: An Uncensored History of America's Top Secret Military Base* (New York: Back Bay Books, 2011), 17.

"Major Marcel, did you . . .": Berlitz and Moore, 63.

"I saw a lot . . .": ibid.

"Whatever it was . . .": ibid.

"If another military group . . .": ibid., 69.

"It was not . . .": ibid., 65.

"[I] was told . . .": ibid., 67.

"less-interesting metallic debris": ibid., 68.

"Then they allowed . . .": ibid.

"the actual wreckage . . .": ibid.

"So you're saying . . .": ibid., 68–69.

"One thing that I want. . .": ibid., 68.

"I repeat, the material . . .": ibid., 69.

"They were like human . . .": ibid., 54–55.

"No, I don't exactly recall . . .": ibid., 57.

"Roswell Hardware Man . . .": "Roswell Hardware Man and Wife Report Disk Seen," *Roswell Daily Record*, July 8, 1947, 1.

"all of a sudden . . .": ibid.

"slight swishing sound": ibid.

"at about ten minutes . . .": ibid.

"one of the most respected . . .": ibid.

"at the base for about," Berlitz and Moore, 83.

## Chapter 14: Is This What Really Happened at Roswell?

"Extraordinary claims require . . .": "The Sagan Standard: Extraordinary Claims Require Extraordinary Evidence," Effectiviology.com, https://effectiviology.com/sagan-standard-extra-claims-require-extraordinary-evidence/.

## Chapter 15: Real, Or Fake?

"On 07 July, 1947 . . .": "Majestic 12," FBI Records: The Vault, https://vault.fbi.gov/Majestic%2012.

"drop on a doorstep . . .": Carl Sagan, *The Demon Haunted World: Science as a Candle in the Dark* (New York: Ballantine Books, 1996), 91.

"fabricated and completely bogus": "Majestic 12."

"That's a [gosh-durned] . . .": Sobel, 94.

## Chapter 16: Can a Five-Year-Old Remember All This?

"I'm here in Kansas City . . .": "Interview of Gerald Anderson 07/24/1991," US National Archives, https://www.youtube.com/watch?v=ivaWnbKsBkM.

"So with that . . .": ibid.

"What did [the creatures]": ibid.

"a bluish tint": ibid.

"like a cut": ibid.

"three boys and two girls": ibid.

"Would this make . . .": ibid.

"Get away! Get away!": ibid.

"This is a military secret": ibid.

"Clearly this was not . . .": Sobel, 94.

"exclusive testimony . . ." Don Berliner and Stanton T. Friedman, *Crash at Corona* (New York: Marlowe & Company, 1992), front cover.

"new evidence of . . .": ibid.

## Chapter 17: A Top Secret Group of Nine?

"It was the blips, see?" Pflock, *Roswell: Inconvenient Facts,* 72.

"The Group of Nine": Kevin D. Randle and Mark Rodeghier, "Frank Kaufmann Reconsidered," *IUR*, Fall 2002, 8.

"the radar screen . . .": Pflock, *Roswell: Inconvenient Facts,* 73.

"On an old ranch road . . .": ibid.

"split open spaceship": ibid.

"That's the one . . .": Kevin D. Randle and Donald R. Schmitt, *The Truth about the UFO Crash at Roswell,* New York: M Evans & Co., 1994, 25.

"We were all talking . . .": ibid., 11.

"normal": Pflock, *Roswell: Inconvenient Facts,* 73.

"paler grayish skin": ibid.

"The medical MPs": ibid., 74.

"Some people there . . .": ibid.

"Maybe": ibid.

"He might have taken . . .": ibid., 75.

"Know what else . . .": ibid.

"Object Down . . .": Randle and Rodeghier, 8.

"Recovery, Flying Discs . . .": ibid., 19.

"The craft recovered . . .": ibid.

"But every time . . .": ibid, 18.

"If what he said . . .": ibid.

"In 1947, and for years . . .": Pflock, *Roswell: Inconvenient Facts,* 81.

## Chapter 18: The Truth, or a Tall Tale?

"in case something . . .": Pflock, *Roswell: Inconvenient Facts,* 28.

"It resembled . . .": ibid., 30.

"Don't move from here . . .": Karl T. Pflock, "Star Witness: The Mortician of Roswell Breaks His Code of Silence," *Omni Magazine*, Fall 1995, 103.

"Bring him back here": ibid.

"Look mister. . . ": ibid.

"I'm a civilian . . .": ibid.

"Somebody will be . . .": ibid.

"Sir, he would make . . . ibid.

"Get him out . . .": ibid.

"Glenn! Get out . . .": ibid., 104.

"But I don' know . . .": ibid.

"Well, I'll tell you why": ibid.

"Guard them with . . .": ibid., 105.

"Maybe that's what . . .": ibid.

"To tell you the truth . . .": ibid.

"Return to sender" and "Deceased": Pflock, *Roswell: Inconvenient Facts,* 31.

## Chapter 19: Can a Ufologist Fool Himself?

"Yes!" James W. Moseley and Karl T. Pflock, *Shockingly Close to the Truth: Confessions of a Grave-Robbing Ufologist* (Amherst, NY: Prometheus Books, 2002), 20.

"My brain wouldn't . . .": ibid., 21.

"Serious Stuff": ibid.

"objectivity, competence . . .": ibid., 16.

"alleged recollections of witnesses": Pflock, *Roswell: Inconvenient Facts,* 122.

"big circus labeled UFO": Moseley and Pflock, 22.

"Consider everything . . .": ibid., 261.

"If someone else . . .": Pflock, *Roswell: Inconvenient Facts,* 127.

"Would you buy . . .": ibid.

"No way!": ibid.

"If Glenn said . . .": ibid.

"I was convinced . . .": ibid., 129.

"Once again it appears . . .": Paul McCarthy, "The Case of the Missing Nurses," *Omni,* Fall 1995, 108–109.

"saucer logic": Moseley and Pflock, 313.

"flash recollection": Pflock, *Roswell: Inconvenient Facts,* 131.

"I promised her . . .": ibid., 134.

"Baloney by any other . . .": ibid.

"Because of an overwhelming . . .": ibid.

## Chapter 20: Wait . . . Is *This* What Really Happened at Roswell?

"UFO Capital of the World": Sobel, 97.

"I think 99.9 percent . . .": ibid.

"Is Roswell the . . .": ibid.

"Maybe .005 percent": ibid.

"THIS IS THE FBI . . .": Kevin D. Randle, *Crash: When UFOs Fall From The Sky: A History of Famous Incidents, Conspiracies, And Cover-Ups* (Franklin Lakes, NJ: New Page Books, 2010), 87.

## Chapter 21: An "Alien Autopsy" . . . for Real?

"It's no different . . .": Nathalie Lagerfeld, "How an Alien Autopsy Hoax Captured the World's Imagination for a Decade," *Time,* June 24, 2016, https://time.com/4376871/alien-autopsy-hoax-history/.

"restoring the *Mona Lisa* . . .": ibid.

## Chapter 22: Roswell: Case Closed, or Not?

"We're confident once the report . . . ": "Air Force Report on Roswell Events," https://c-span.org/video/?87217-1/air-force-report-roswell-events.

"Today we are releasing . . .": ibid.

"As we age . . .": ibid.

"probably test dummies . . .": ibid.

"high altitude research . . .": ibid.

"most likely a combination . . .": ibid.

## Chapter 24: A Case of Wishful Thinking?

"child of earth": Les Carpenter, "The Curious Case of the Alien in the Photo and the Mystery That Took Years to Solve," *Guardian*, September 30, 2017, https//the guardian.com/science/2017/Sep/30/alien-photo-Rosewell-new-mexico-mystery.

"When I saw . . .": ibid.

"It's nothing like . . .": ibid.

"That's what I saw in 1947": ibid.

"We have the smoking gun . . .": Robert Sheaffer, "The 'Roswell Slides' Fiasco: Ufology's Biggest Black Eye," *Skeptical Inquirer*, September/October 2015, 30.

"It certainly is . . .": David J. Hogan, *UFO FAQ: All That's Left to Know About Roswell, Aliens, Whirling Discs, and Flying Saucers* (Milwaukee: Backbeat Books, 2016), 230.

"We've had everyone . . .": Sheaffer, 31.

"MUMMIFIED BODY . . .": ibid., 32.

"You folks solved . . .": ibid.

"At the time . . .": Hogan, 230.

"overly trusting": Sheaffer, 32.

"still open to debate": ibid.

"It's the biggest . . .": ibid., 30.

"Our revels here . . .": Pflock, *Roswell: Inconvenient Facts*, 243.

## Chapter 25: Why So Secretive?

"I don't think much . . .": Keith Kloor, "UFOs Won't Go Away," *Issues in Science and Technology* 35, no. 3, Spring 2019, https://issues.org/ufos-wont-go-away/.

"It was behaving . . .": Victor Tangermann, "Navy Pilot Describes Bizzare 'Tic Tac' UFO Encounter He Filmed," Futurism.com, https://futurism.com/navy-pilot-bizzare-ufo-encounter.

"a cube encasing a sphere": Helen Cooper, Ralph Blumenthal, and Leslie Kean, "'Wow, What Is That?' Navy Pilots Report Unexplained Flying Objects," *New York Times*, May 27, 2019, A14.

"They're all going . . .": "Statement by Department of Defense on the Release of Historic Navy Videos," https://www.navair.navy.mil/foia/documents.

"Look at that thing . . .": ibid.

"The UAP issue . . .": Gideon Lewis-Krause, "How the Pentagon Started Taking U.F.O.S Seriously," *New Yorker*, April 30, 2021, https://www.newyorker.com/magazine/2021/05/10/how-the-pentagon-started-taking-ufos-seriously?source=search_google_dsa_paid&gclid=

Cj0KCQiAnuGNBhCPARIsACbnLzrxzm7aQ7L5zd9zjk
DYBxtjCxFjXjkjwo5ofG3vUJ53CouQf0RMCs8aAnFEEALw_wcB.

"incursions into our . . .": Leonard David, "Experts Weight In on Pentagon UFO Report," scientificamerican.com/article/experts-weigh-in-on-pentagon-ufo-report/.

"detect, analyze . . ." Office of the Director of National Intelligence, "Preliminary Assessment: Unidentified Aerial Phenomena," dni.gov/ODNI/documents/assessments/Preliminary-Assessment-UAP-20210625.pdf.

## Chapter 26: The Truth?

"near misses": Office of the Director of National Intelligence, "Preliminary Assessment: Unidentified Aerial Phenomena."

"radar, infra-red . . .": ibid.

"pose[d] a challenge . . .": ibid.

"Look, the truth is . . .": "Obama Talks UFOs on James Corden," https://www.youtube.com/watch?v=tKSyYTerGTI.

# ☆ PHOTOGRAPH AND ☆ ILLUSTRATION CREDITS

Worth Star-Telegram Collection, Special Collections, The University of Texas at Arlington Libraries; 36: Courtesy, Fort Worth Star-Telegram Collection, Special Collections, The University of Texas at Arlington Libraries; 37: Richard Cummins/Alamy Stock Photo; 38: Department of Justice; 44: Library of Congress; 45: Library of Congress; 46: National Archives; 47: National Archives; 48: U.S. Air Force; 51: Candace Fleming; 56: Dave Mathias/The Denver Post via Getty Images; 63: National Archives; 64: Eric Rohmann; 65: U.S. Air Force; 66: National Archives; 67: National Archives; 70: Pictorial Press Ltd/Alamy Stock Photo; 71: Alvin Quinn/AP Images; 72: National Archives; 74: National Archives; 75: Library of Congress; 76: National Archives; 77: National Archives; 83: Retro AdArchives/Alamy Stock Photo; 84: Library of Congress; 86: Courtesy of the NICAP; 88: U.S. Air Force; 91: National Archives; 92: National Archives; 94: Photo 12/Alamy Stock Photo; 95: Eric Rohmann; 106: Candace Fleming; 129: Department of Justice; 136–137: Eric Rohmann; 142: National Archives; 145: Eric Rohmann; 147: Eric Rohmann; 149: Library of Congress; 157: International

# ☆ INDEX ☆

Page numbers in *italics* refer to illustrations.

# ☆ ACKNOWLEDGMENTS ☆

I am deeply indebted to my patient and enthusiastic editor, Lisa Sandell, who pivoted to this unexpected project with poise and good cheer.

Thanks, too, to the whole wonderful Scholastic team, especially Lizette, Alex, and Emily, who always make me look so good.

For bringing his expertise and enthusiasm to the vetting of this manuscript, I owe many thanks to Dr. Greg Eghigian, professor of history at Penn State University and expert on UFO phenomenon.

Much appreciation goes to Dr. Mark Rodeghier, science director of the Center for UFO Studies, and to Sam Maranto, State Director of the Illinois Mutual UFO Network, for answering questions, replying to requests, and providing so many unexpected insights.

There are never enough thanks for Eric Rohmann—for listening, photographing, braving snakes and spiders, and generously contributing his artistic talents. I'm so grateful for our partnership.

# ☆ ABOUT THE AUTHOR ☆

Candace Fleming is the versatile and acclaimed author of more than twenty books for children and young adults, including *The Curse of the Mummy: Uncovering Tutankhamun's Tomb*; *The Rise and Fall of Charles Lindbergh*, winner of the YALSA Award for Excellence in Nonfiction for Young Adults; the Sibert Award–winner *Honeybee: The Busy Life of* Apis Mellifera; *Los Angeles Times* Book Prize–winner and Sibert Honor Book *The Family Romanov: Murder, Rebellion, and the Fall of the Russian Empire*; the critically acclaimed *Amelia Lost: The Life and Disappearance of Amelia Earhart*; *Boston Globe–Horn Book* Award-winning biography, *The Lincolns*; the bestselling picture book, *Muncha! Muncha! Muncha!*; and the beloved *Boxes for Katje*.